BEWITCHED

TITANIA'S BOOK
OF LOVE SPELLS
TITANIA HARDIE

BEWITCHED

TITANIA'S BOOK
OF LOVE SPELLS
TITANIA HARDIE
PHOTOGRAPHS
BY SARA MORRIS

STEWART, TABORI & CHANG
NEW YORK, NEW YORK

The author and publisher would like to dedicate this book
to Martin Doyle, 1948-1997, and his beloved Solange:

"All other things to their destruction draw,
Only our love hath no decay;
This, no tomorrow hath, nor yesterday,
Running it never runs from us away,
But truly keeps his first, last, everlasting day."

John Donne

Text copyright © 1997 by Titania Hardie
Photographs copyright © 1997 by Sara Morris
Layout and design copyright © 1997 by Quadrille Publishing Limited
Designed by Johnson Banks

First published in 1997 by Quadrille Publishing Limited
Alhambra House, 27–31 Charing Cross Road, London WC2H 0LS, England

Published in 1997 and distributed in the U.S. by Stewart, Tabori and Chang,
a division of U.S. Media Holdings, Inc. 115 West 18th Street, New York, NY 10011

Distributed in Canada by General Publishing Company Ltd.
30 Lesmill Road, Don Mills, Ontario, Canada M3B 2T6

Library of Congress Cataloging-in-Publication Data

Hardie, Titania.
    Bewitched: Titania's book of love spells / by Titania Hardie;
photographs by Sara Morris.

        p. cm.
        ISBN 1-55670-652-9 (hardcover)
        1. Magic. 2. Love—Miscellanea. 1. Title
    BF1623.L6H37   1997
    133.4'42—DC21   97-8685

Printed and bound by Arnoldo Mondadori Editore spa, Verona, Italy

10 9 8 7 6 5 4 3 2 1

An introduction to the magic of love ♥ THE SUBJECT OF

LOVE IS THE INSPIRATION OF POETS AND PAINTERS; it is usually somewhere at the heart of the dramas we watch, the songs we listen to, the books we read. Questions regarding the success and failure of love affairs fuel the conversations we have with friends; perhaps, too, considerations of love are involved in the choice of perfumes we wear and the clothes we buy. And yet, even the wisest minds are at a loss to understand why and how love occurs between any two people. We have no more idea why one seemingly perfect union goes awry and another—perhaps the pairing of an apparently odd couple—survives every test of affection.

♥ Is LOVE, THEN, CHANCE? In part, surely, yes: it must be chance that determines many meetings. Apart from the likelihood of meeting in a workplace or via a friend's friend, how many chance encounters have brought lovers together in unlikely places, on opposite sides of the globe, in lines or gatherings where neither would usually be? And, are love's workings a mystery? Again, at least in part, yes: for although psychologists will take pains to rationalize how love flourishes, or why it takes root at all (and certainly what personality types are doomed to repeated heartache), still so many answers evade a clinical approach. Over and over, for no obvious reason, the most unlikely couples are drawn to one another, or, sadly, seemingly ideally suited people fail in love because one doesn't quite live up to the expectations of the other. ♥ SO MAGIC ENTERS THE SCENE, AND WHAT COULD BE MORE FITTING? Shakespeare often turned to magic potions and rituals to move the drama on—many other poets look to elixirs, magic, myth, and mystery to resolve their tales of love. Couples I know who seem as delighted and surprised by one another twenty and more years after their first encounter could be truthfully said to have "bewitched" each other. They speak of the "magic" of their relationship, of the transfiguring qualities of a special union. Such blessed lovers have seemingly discovered love's alchemy—the power of love to take base emotions and weave from them a golden, transcendent state.

♥ THESE IDEAS ARE MORE THAN MERELY FIGURES OF SPEECH; THE POSSIBILITY OF THIS MAGICAL LOVE IS THERE FOR EVERYONE. In this book there are rituals handed down through generations that show how to meet, secure, and enthrall a lover. Some are playful, some funny, some poetic, some very potent indeed; some require that we look inward, to see if previous misfortune in love can be resolved by a simple change of approach—the adopting of a new and positive attitude. ♥ CERTAINLY THERE IS A RIGHT STATE OF MIND FOR BEING LOVED. This begins by being at least modestly happy with oneself, for if we don't love ourselves, how can we expect anyone to find us lovable? If we are riddled with self-doubt and lack of confidence, how can we expect to be relaxed enough to develop the love relationships we attract in the first place? Those considered lucky in love have a special spirit and sense of self-worth which can make them more magnetic in a crowded room than any supermodel or pop star. When you are just falling in love, it is often the case that you give off such an enigmatic radiance that others are attracted to you too; yet when you are bereft of love, you emit a signal of insecurity, brittleness, desperation, which makes others avoid you almost instinctively. But this need not be. . . . ♥ IF SOMETHING IN OUR BODY LANGUAGE AND PSYCHE ENABLES OTHERS TO READ AND UNDERSTAND WHAT WE ARE LOOKING FOR; if a room full of unfamiliar people respond to the signals we give out, then we must learn how to make use of this in love courting. Perhaps this is what love magic is all about: through ritual, the use of oils and aromas, and by putting ourselves into an almost hypnotic state, we can strengthen and improve our body language and courting signals to attract more positive love. Better still, through magical games and ceremonies we can heighten our awareness of what it is that keeps a relationship happy, and, hopefully, even learn how to evolve the relationship to greater levels of closeness.

Working magic ❤ To make magic work you must have a very strong and

CONCENTRATED MIND. Magical transformation is realized by fixing your sights on a matter and drawing it to you, as powerfully as a magnet. Sometimes actual physical properties are brought into play through the use of herbs, potions, and aromas; always, there is a ritual associated with this which makes use of the "wish power." This is a very viable source and not a plaything; I well remember my sensible mother (herself the daughter of a white witch) urging me to be careful what I wished for lest I should make my wish come true! In other words, choose your goals carefully, and think about the repercussions for yourself, as well as others, of the magic you set in motion. It is not playing fair to poach another person's beloved (although there is nothing wrong with using a little magic to help someone finally let go of a relationship which is palpably over, as long as this is genuinely the case). If the aims of your spells are purely selfish, you will assuredly come to regret your interference, for witchcraft embraces the philosophy of deeds being revisited upon the worker to the power of three: loving, positive, unselfish deeds and thoughts are repaid three times over; likewise, efforts to enchain another against his or her will will bring misery in greater measure to the person who works the spell. ❤ THIS SAID, AND ASSUMING YOUR MOTIVES STAND THE TEST OF INTEGRITY, IT IS VITAL TO MAKE YOUR MAGIC SUCCEED. In my previous book, *Hocus Pocus,* the aim of which was to introduce magic for a wide range of areas in everyday life, it was not necessary to concentrate specially on a particular regime of preparation for the spells. However, for specific love magic, thorough preparation before working any individual spell cannot be recommended too strongly. In the arena of love you are dealing with a sensitive part of your own and another's psyche: it is imperative to cleanse away negativity, pledge your motives, and minimize (even remove) imbalances in your own personality such as possessiveness and obsessive tendencies. This is best achieved by color breathing, a simple but powerful technique of drawing color warmth and healing rays into your own being, and then enveloping the thoughts you send magically in these special colors to ensure their best possible reception at the other end.

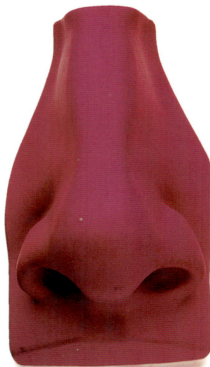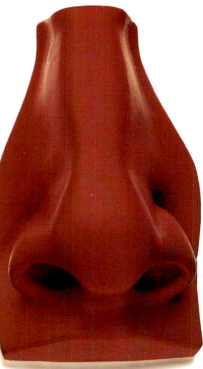

Color breathing ♥ THE USE OF COLOR IN MAGIC IS AS OLD AS THE SUBJECT ITSELF. The

great Indian, Chinese, Arabic, and Western objectives of alchemy, which were originally concerned with medicine rather than the making of gold, employed the use of color tone in the hope of altering the vibratory rates of base metals. Certainly, the effect of color on the individual psyche cannot be doubted, and we are beginning to understand the use of color in therapy for altering the mood of distressed and disturbed souls. For instance, subjecting a stressed person to the color red irritates them still further, while putting a hyperactive child into a pink room will calm him or her down. ♥ MANY MAGICAL RITUALS INVOLVE DRENCHING THE SENSES IN COLOR AS A PRECURSOR TO WORKING THE MAGIC AND SENDING THE POWERFUL THOUGHT FORCES. This requires a careful selection of shade to suit the job to be done, some of which is dictated and some of which can be personal to give the magic a sense of "signature" for the worker. In other words, if you are dealing with the area of healing, you should work in the blue/green color field, which is known to have a beneficial effect on the body's self-healing process, but select a shade of blue or green to which you personally respond well. ♥ IN MATTERS OF THE HEART THERE IS NO COLOR QUITE LIKE PINK: IT HAS AN AGE-OLD ASSOCIATION WITH LOVE. The more purple there is in the pink, the more passion you are injecting. When you add yellow you add intellect; blue adds loyalty, and red, lust. ♥ TO SEND GREATER FORCE WITH YOUR LOVE MAGIC, LEARN TO BREATHE IN THE COLOR YOU ARE WORKING WITH. Light the candle(s) of your chosen color(s) (usually, one color prescribed for the spell, and one color that is your own "signature" choice—see appendix), then inhale the feeling of the color along with any scent that might already be in the candle. You do this by vividly imagining the color entering your lungs, chest, head, and heart and then gradually spreading the sense of the color down through your body, ending up right at your toes. By doing this you are altering your own "vibratory rate" and giving yourself up to the power of the colored light. For this reason, when you want to protect yourself or anyone else you breathe in pure white light, which contains all the properties of all the colors and represents the full power of the light rather than any break in the spectrum. ♥ THE COLORS HAVE A SPECIFIC CORRESPONDENCE TO NUMBERS AND STRATEGY. This is the list you should consider when choosing an appropriate hue: COLOR ONE: *Initiating things: flame red.* COLOR TWO: *Pairing off: salmon pink.* COLOR THREE: *Groups (crowds): amber.* COLOR FOUR: *Marriage and families: blue/indigo.* COLOR FIVE: *Passion and action: purple/wisteria.* COLOR SIX: *Perfect love: rose pink.* COLOR SEVEN: *Analysis: brick.* COLOR EIGHT: *Material stability: bronze/sunshine yellow.* COLOR NINE: *Forgiveness: olive/green.* COLOR TEN: *Master associations: silver.* COLOR ELEVEN: *Achieving your destiny: black and white.*

Scented magic ♥ I HAVE TOUCHED HERE ON THE SUBJECT OF SCENT IN CANDLES AND

INHALING IT AS PART OF THE CLEANSING, STRENGTHENING RITUAL. However, the whole business of scent also has a significant influence on our psychological awareness and the signals we emit to others; this awareness fuels the multimillion-dollar perfume industry, after all. But designer fragrances had an antecedent in floral and herbal washes (indeed, the name *lavandula,* or lavender, comes from the Latin "to wash," as no self-respecting Roman omitted this powerful ingredient from his ablutions). In days past, when streets, houses, and people were less sanitary, anyone who understood the art of fragrancing their hair and body with the oils extracted from herbs and flowers was deemed to have magical powers over the opposite sex. Thus, used with knowledge, scent is a vital component in the effects of the magic we work. ♥ SOMETIMES IT IS EASIEST TO CHOOSE CANDLES THAT ARE ALREADY SCENTED WITH WHICH TO WORK YOUR MAGIC: lavender to cheer the senses and excite the passions, rose to purify the environment and the psychological state of the speller, rosemary to wake up the brain and engage the mind in high gear, melissa (lemon balm) to calm a raging anger or settle nerves, geranium to balance your mood, and so on. It is also worth sprinkling drops of aromatic oils on the magical altars in your home, on lightbulb rings, or burning them in special burners so that the scent really permeates the physical space. There is nothing better than bathing in a cleansing bath scented with a carefully chosen essential oil to magnify the force of your magic. Even if you are allergic to perfume, it is probably the chemical used to synthesize scent that is the problem; the subtle use of true essential oils—or a light strewing of the herbs themselves—will be an entirely different story. In any case, consult the appendix and decide which scent matches your need, then experiment a little. Releasing powerful fragrance into the air is a good forerunner to creating a magic circle, which is also worth taking the trouble to do for love spells.

The magic circle ❤

THERE ARE MANY DESCRIPTIONS OF THE KINDS OF CIRCLE YOU MIGHT USE FOR MAGIC PURPOSES, MOST EVOLVING FROM DRUIDIC TRADITIONS. But since the purpose of certain Druidic circles was often connected with the macabre ritual of sacrifice for divination, I personally prefer my grandmother's mode of drawing a circle, which is like a liquid pool of light in which one sits to send forth enlightened thoughts. This was a prerequisite in all her workings for healing, and I believe it is essential in love magic also, for a circle is a powerful talisman against negative entities which might otherwise be curious about your magic. Use it first and foremost to protect you from negativity and, secondly, to concentrate and heighten your power. ❤ USE TINY VOTIVE CANDLES, WHICH ARE BY FAR THE SAFEST FOR WORKING INDOORS OR OUT, AND CHOOSE THEIR COLOR AND SCENT AS YOU WISH. On the night of a full moon, stand in the center of the circle you plan to create, and work clockwise, placing the candles at roughly 12-inch intervals to mark out a circle about a yard and a half in diameter. Strew the center of the circle with rose petals (or rose oil if the season does not permit the real article), and in the south of the circle place a small dish of water. When you are ready to start your magic, raise your arms to the moon, which should be in clear view, and draw down her energy and luminosity into your circle. Then, starting in the north part of the circle, light the candles, moving around clockwise so that you remain in the center as the flames grow in power. Once the candles are lit, you must imagine a beam of white light cleansing you, the circle, and the room in which you work: then send this beam on to the person who is the recipient of your magic-working, so that you are sending him or her your honesty and positivity as well. Concentrate your energy until you can feel it like a tangible force within the circle. When you are sure of its electrical current, you are ready to unleash the force with the spell, which you can now work, chosen for its individual purpose.

Safety note ❤

Throughout this book there are spells that involve burning candles. When doing so, please make sure that you obey the following safety rules: always put a candle in a holder before lighting; make sure there is nothing nearby that might catch fire, such as curtains which might be blown by the wind; never leave lit candles unattended.

LOOKING FOR
LOVE

1

This chapter is dedicated to anyone for whom the night sky of love is without one special star. If being footloose and fancy free has lost its appeal, these spells provide the perfect way to knock on the celestial door and announce to those within hearing that you are there. Begin any individual spell with your magic circle, choose a light rose or flame-red candle to breathe in to initiate things, then fasten the belt on your broomstick for a voyage of discovery . . . .

Honoring self ❤ A SPELL TO DO BEFORE ALL OTHERS. This is the best spell to begin all magic workings and a simple one to perform. It is a good spell to use in tandem with more sophisticated rituals.

YOU WILL NEED

A photo of yourself; thin embroidery ribbons; a silver photo frame; several white votive candles

MOON PHASE: *Full moon*

❤ THE WHOLE POINT OF THIS SPELL IS THAT IT IS YOUR OWN "AUTOGRAPH," TO PRECEDE ALL OTHER SPELLS. Before you start, make yourself an altar or special place within your home that emanates radiance and love. When making your altar, choose flowers, colors, and symbols that are particularly appealing to you. ❤ ON THE NIGHT OF A FULL MOON, trim your photo into a heart shape and lovingly embroider it with ribbons around the edge. Choose colors that please you and that give your work a personal sense of symbolism. Chant as you work, singing a little personal song about love that you like or that you make up for yourself. ❤ WHEN YOUR HANDIWORK IS COMPLETE, PLACE IT IN A FRAME AND THEN ON YOUR ALTAR. Light a candle next to the image every night until the following full moon: soon after, your luck in love will be assured.

Address to the evening star ♥

A SPELL OF ENTREATY. This ancient spell evolves from the practice of manifesting the benevolent spirit of the love goddess and humbly, though confidently, asking her to bestow upon you a worthy love. The evening star, Venus, is her special attendant, so pay homage with a sincere heart, as though you had her very ear.

YOU WILL NEED

3 yards violet-colored satin ribbon and 3 white; a lock of your hair, trimmed at sundown; rose oil; 3 violet-colored votive candles and 3 white, in appropriate holders

MOON PHASE: *Full*

♥ WORKING ON THE FULL MOON TO ENSURE THAT THE TIDES THAT RULE OUR EMOTIONS ARE HIGH, MAKE A SIX-POINTED STAR. Make the violet ribbon into an equal-sided triangle; do the same with the white ribbon, then lay one triangle upside-down over the other to form a six-pointed star. In the center of the star place a lock of your hair sprinkled with a little rose oil. ♥ WHEN THE EVENING STAR HAS RISEN (USUALLY JUST AFTER SUNDOWN), kneel before it with the votive candles cradled in your open palms and say: *"Venus, friend to earthly lovers, With your gifts to cheer the heart, May you now a friend uncover, Who in romance takes my part, Find a mate by love unfetter'd, By whose light my love is better'd. So mote it be."* In deep reverence for the goodness and warmth of growing love, and by the light of the star, take each candle and place one on a matching point of the ribboned star, lighting first that to the west, the direction from which the wind blows, to bring the springtime and flowers.

♥ WHEN ALL ARE LIT, SIT IN THE MIDST OF THE STARLIGHT AND REPEAT THE WORDS. Imagine your life irradiated with a new, gentle, soundly growing love, and make a pledge to cherish all people more when this love enters your life. Let the candles burn for about an hour, then take the ribbons and use them to tie the lock of your hair. Place this special token somewhere where it can catch the starlight, and wait for one moon cycle (28 days). Thereafter, love will surely triumph.

A solstice prayer ♥ A SUNRISE OFFERING TO THE LOVE GODDESS ON THE SOLSTICE,

FOLLOWED BY THE PLANTING OF A WHITE ROSE. Legend has it that on the day Venus was born roses first appeared in a showery breeze and accompanied her journey to shore in a shell, a moment interpreted beautifully by Botticelli in his famous painting *"The Birth of Venus."* The solstice is, by tradition, the celestial moment of change; their dates are Summer: June 21; Winter: December 21. Or use the equinox; Spring: March 21; Autumn: September 21.

YOU WILL NEED

2 small pieces of paper; one white rose bush (miniature will be fine if you have only a small patio or tiny garden); a metal watering can (green or silver is best, but not black); a flower press for preserving the first bloom; 1 white or pale rose candle

MOON PHASE: *Full*

♥ ON THE MORNING OF WHICHEVER SOLSTICE YOU SELECT FOR YOUR PRAYER YOU MUST WAKE WITH THE FIRST BEAM OF SUNSHINE AND BOW YOUR HEAD TO ITS LIFE-GIVING WARMTH. Quickly write your name on one of the pieces of paper, and take your rose bush into the garden, or onto your patio or balcony, to plant it. ♥ OPEN YOUR ARMS TO THE GODDESS, FOR IT IS HER WHOM YOU ADDRESS RATHER THAN THE SUN ITSELF, and tell her you plant her flower to honor her and bring her charms and gifts of love into your home. With great solemnity and care, plant the rose bush, placing the piece of paper with your name on it under the roots as a petition. (As an avid rose gardener I am bound to urge you to put in plenty of well-rotted horse manure—the very best fertilizer for roses—as you plant it, and to water the ground or the pot thoroughly to prepare it for your plant; in this way both your plant and your spell will thrive.) Now raise your arms to the heavens and call upon Venus and her attendants to favor you with a wonderful love. Float the other piece of paper, with your name written on it, in the watering can and water in the rose. Replenish the can and water the rose every day until it is well established and flowers spring forth.

♥ AT THE APPROPRIATE SEASON YOUR ROSE WILL BLOSSOM AND WITH IT LOVE WILL BE BORN. Preserve the first bud, pressed, for the goddess alone, and place it on a kind of altar, with a white or pale rose candle. Flowers must afterward be freely picked and given to others who need love in their lives.

As above so below ❤

A SECOND SPELL OF ENTREATY. On this occasion a living star is created as a mirror of the cosmos, at the heart of which is the glowing light of your own being looking for its soulmate. Though it requires more patience than the "Address to the evening star," it is a beautiful and powerful spell which also provides an aesthetic treat for your garden or windowbox.

YOU WILL NEED

A selection of flower seeds including pansies, daisies, dwarf candytuft, petunias, and phlox (if you have trouble finding any of these, substitute by all means, but be sure to choose a flower that will be of height and flowering time similar to the others); a handful of small shells; a photograph of you looking happy; a flame-colored dinner candle

MOON PHASE: *Very new*

❤ WHEN SPRING FIRST SCENTS THE AIR WITH THE PROMISE OF WARMTH AND GROWTH, walk into your garden, or to a window facing onto new green growth, and bow to the four corners of the globe, and the four elements of being—earth, sky, flame, and water. ❤ MEASURE OUT A FIVE-POINTED STAR IN EARTH, either in a small seed tray, if small must be your scale, or in a sunny corner of your garden or patio. Use the tip of a trowel to make a furrow deep enough to sow lightly the seeds of your living star, and mark every intersecting line with shells, sacred to the sea from which Venus sprang. ❤ BEFORE SOWING THE SEEDS, PLACE A PHOTOGRAPH OF YOURSELF AT THE HEART OF THE STAR, and in your own words ask that love visit special blessings on your soul. Atop the photo place the candle. Now sow the seeds, one variety along each line of the star, singing cheerfully as you work—for Venus and her attendants cannot resist sweet music! When your gardening is complete, water the seeds with the tenderest of feelings, in full awareness that you are helping to call life forth from them. At completion, light the candle for the first vigil while the seedlings grow. Imagine that a celestial star is now stirring with an awareness of you, bringing new life and love to you at full flowering. ❤ WHAT REMAINS IS FOR YOU TO TEND YOUR GARDEN CAREFULLY, pruning seedlings out as necessary to maintain the lines of the star. On each day of the new moon, and when you water, light the candle for ten or fifteen minutes. ❤ ALTHOUGH IT WILL TAKE SEVERAL WEEKS, NEW ATTRACTIONS WILL BUD IN YOUR LIFE; and when your star flowers, so too a new love will blossom forth. As this happens, bow again to the corners of your garden (big or small), and thank Venus and her attendants for their care.

The band of violets ♥ MOST BEAUTIFUL OF THE MANY LEGENDS OF THE VIOLET IS

THAT OF CUPID, WHO LOOSES HIS BOW IN LOVE UPON A STARRY MAIDEN; but, missing its mark, his arrow falls instead upon a patch of milk-white violets, gradually turning them in rings from the center outward to the more familiar, passionate purple we know today. This features in Shakespeare's *A Midsummer Night's Dream,* when Oberon instructs Puck to collect the juice of the flower and sprinkle it on Titania's eyelids so that she will fall in love with the first person she sees on waking. To loose your fiery arrow into the darkness and find a lover, follow this adaptation of the spell. *"Yet marked I where the bolt of Cupid fell. It fell upon a little western flower—Before, milk-white; now, purple with love's wound."*

YOU WILL NEED

⅓ cup violet flowers (dried or fresh); 2 oz. goat's or sheep's milk; a small candle, either violet-colored or violet-scented; a nosegay of fresh violets for working into a band for the hair or into a necklace

MOON PHASE: *Full*

♥ ON THE VERY FIRST NIGHT OF A NEW MOON, steep the ⅓ cup of violet flowers in the milk for an hour. While they are steeping, make a circle of the fresh violets with the candle in the center and light it, saying: *"Cupid loose your fiery brand, May this flower be Love's command!"* Now, in front of the glowing candle, bathe your face with the violet-scented milk (don't be alarmed: it makes an excellent skin tonic). Picture yourself seated in the midst of a ring of white flowers gradually turning purple with the onset of love; imagine love coloring your own life in this way. Complete the spell by weaving the violets into a daisy-chain-like band, big enough for a necklace or a chaplet for your hair. ♥ ON THE DAY FOLLOWING YOUR MAGIC WORKING, WEAR THE FLOWERS ALL DAY, repeating the words above softly at odd intervals. By the time of the full moon you should be fending off interested parties, and within the month you will have met someone very special indeed. **If violets are truly scarce you could use just one flower, placed in front of the candle, and put it into a locket which you would then wear in place of the garland of flowers. This has the added advantage of becoming a long-term love token.**

Two talismans ♥

AN INDIAN LOVE SPELL. Saris and Nandini, well-loved and respected friends from Madras in Southern India, taught me this spell, which they swear by for drawing a potent love into your life.

YOU WILL NEED

A small handcrafted wooden box you have made yourself, or one you like the look and feel of and into which you must pour your thoughts and feelings of hope; a few drops of sandalwood oil; some clippings of your hair; some of your nail filings; a precious blend of Indian spices: a good pinch each of cumin, coriander, and cardamom and a few strands of saffron; a length of gold-colored cord

MOON PHASE: *Waxing*

♥ ON THE EVENING OF A GROWING MOON, place into a box that has been scented with sandalwood oil a few of your hairs and nail filings, along with the sacred spices mentioned above. Offer the treasure up to the evening sky, and ask that many precious new senses enter your life, not least of which is a special love. ♥ NOW VIEW YOURSELF AS SOMEONE PRECIOUS, TREASURED, AND FEEL THE ENERGIES OF THE SPICES ADDING NEW ZEST TO YOUR SECRET DESIRES. Tie the box up with the cord, and, each night of the growing moon, touch it again with reverence until your admirer appears.

A tinker's love spell ♥

THIS SPELL WAS TOLD TO MY GRANDMOTHER by a tinker's daughter.

YOU WILL NEED

A personal symbol struck from metal (see page 112); a sprig of rosemary tied with rose-colored ribbon; a box in which to keep your talisman (made by you, however crudely, and preferably heart-shaped)

MOON PHASE: *Brand new*

♥ MAKE YOUR TALISMAN USING THE METAL CHARM, the rosemary, and ribbon in a form that you find pleasing. For fourteen nights, while the moon grows, empower your talisman: hold the objects up to the moon, and draw its light and reassuring face, which watches you while you sleep, into your world of dreams. Every night, after the empowering, place the objects in your treasure box and put it under your pillow or bed. ♥ IN A FORTNIGHT YOUR LOVE WILL APPEAR.

The zodiac wheel ♥ ANOTHER PERSONAL TALISMAN. This spell, like "Honoring self," might

be worked before another important spell, or even to boost a love affair that is already in progress. Like the former, it is very potent for those who lack confidence in love, not necessarily to attract a lover but to hold on to one.

YOU WILL NEED

A candle, color of your choice; a small round piece of cardboard; a small velvet pouch, purchased or made by you; an acorn or other nut; a length of ribbon, colored as you prefer

MOON PHASE: *Any*

♥ PREPARE FOR THIS MAGIC-MAKING BY LIGHTING THE CANDLE AND PLAYING SOME MUSIC YOU ENJOY. Write your name and date of birth on the cardboard, with your birth sign and any other astrological information you know, such as ascendant and moon sign. Place the card in the pouch, then hold up your acorn or other nut to the moon, asking that from small beginnings great love may flow. Tie the pouch securely shut with the ribbon—and place it somewhere in your dwelling "on high"—perhaps atop a wardrobe or cabinet, or over a doorway. This complete, you will soon discover you are attracting all kinds of love (not just couple love) into your life, which will give you immense personal magnetism and much all-round popularity.

The silver seal ♥ FOR THIS SPELL YOU MUST FIND A SYMPATHETIC JEWELER WHO CAN MAKE

YOU A CHARM OF YOUR CHOOSING (see page 112 for ideas), beginning their work on a new moon. It does not have to be a large or expensive piece, but something you can treasure forever. When you are first united with your piece of silver you must place it near a bell. Ring this every morning and evening for the duration of that moon to rid the air of all negativity and to promote powerful musical vibrations which draw love into the silver piece and into your home. Now, you will find love enters and remains in your life, whenever you wear your silver. (I know several people who have even worn their piece to their wedding, just to be on the safe side.)

Tears of joy ♥ GYPSY LORE TELLS THAT ONIONS ARE POWERFUL SYMBOLS OF EMOTION BECAUSE

TEARS EMERGE AS YOU CUT ONE. To grow love in the wilderness, a young girl should plant an onion and infuse it with all of her being. In theory it should be watered with all the tears of your past disappointments, but hopefully you will not be reminded of the past too much as you assure your future.

YOU WILL NEED

A small onion, still with its roots; a narrow-necked glass jar, marked with your name and star sign and filled with water;

a terra-cotta pot

MOON PHASE: *Any*

♥ PLACE YOUR BABY ONION INTO THE JAR, WITH THE ROOTS JUST TOUCHING THE WATER'S SURFACE TO ENCOURAGE THE ONION'S GROWTH. Every day, at the same hour, freshen the water and see in your onion's smooth surface a picture of your face, laughing and happy. Now, as it begins to show life, a love will appear; and as it grows more, so too the love will grow steadily. Plant the now shooting onion in a terra-cotta pot, and if your love has a name by now, write it with your own and place it in the earth around the onion bulb. As the onion grows, transplant it to a larger size of pot. The relationship will now grow stronger and stronger.

Moon divinations

♥ TURN YOUR APRON THREE TIMES, LOOKING AT THE NEW MOON; ask for a present or a love and it will surely come to you. ♥ INTERLACING YOUR HANDS ACROSS A NEW MOON, SAY: *"New moon, new moon, I hail thee, Tell me who my love shall be."* Retiring to bed, you will dream of your beloved's face. ♥ ON A CLEAR NIGHT WITH A NEW MOON, GO TO A SPOT WHERE A STONE RESTS NATURALLY IN THE EARTH and, standing upon it, say: *"Oh new moon, all hail thee, If ever I'm to marry man, or man to marry me, Turn his face as fast ye can, that I may his face see. Upon this hallowed night, Let me my true love see."* According to tradition, you will dream of, or meet, the partner of your future sorrows and joys within this moon's reign. ♥ *"Bright is the omen, for love follows soon, on he (she) who will bless, the lovely new moon."* ♥ IF YOU CAN PERCEIVE A NEW MOON THROUGH A SILK HANDKERCHIEF, ASK OF IT: *"New moon, true moon, pray show me, How my true love he (she) may be; In neither best nor worst array, In his (her) garb of everyday, That tomorrow I will know, He (She) who'll through life by me, go."* You must walk backward to bed without a word to a soul in the hope that the next day will reveal your partner in person. ♥ A YOUNG GIRL SHOULD HOLD UP A SILKEN SCARF TO A NEW MOON, through which she will see a vision of as many moons as there will be years before she marries. ♥ IF YOU ARE KISSED ON THE NEWEST MOON OF THE NEW YEAR, within that year your true love will appear and propose marriage. ♥ TRIM A LOCK OF HAIR EVERY MONTH FOR SIX MONTHS ON THE FULL MOON, keep the resulting locks in a silken square of fabric and wish for the love you desire. Within six more moons he/she will declare himself/herself. ♥ IF YOU MEET SOMEONE YOU LIKE, wait until the moon is new before starting the relationship. The new moon is better, to begin affairs of the heart, than the old. ♥ ON THE NIGHT YOU MEET SOMEONE SPECIAL, avoid looking at the moon reflected in a "glass," or mirror, to avoid bringing ill luck upon the blossoming romance.

The Romany candle spell ❤ ONE OF A LONG ROMANY (GYPSY) TRADITION

OF MAGIC RITUALS. This candle spell seeks a lover for an unattached girl or boy, inviting the spark of love to pierce the still night and bring together two well-matched souls. Originally, the spell included the smoking of a cigar to focus the thoughts, because tobacco was held to be potent and magical. This healthier version calls for a toast of spiced wine instead.

YOU WILL NEED

1 yard of red ribbon; a red dinner candle; a small flask of sherry steeped for several days with saffron and cinnamon

MOON PHASE: *Full*

❤ ON THE EARLY EVENING OF A FULL MOON CLOSE TO THE SPRING OR AUTUMN EQUINOX, wrap the ribbon about your brow and tie a bow over your forehead. Gather up your candle and flask of drink, and walk calmly and quietly, as in a procession, to a powerful tree near your dwelling place. Unbind the ribbon from your brow, and place it around the index finger of your dominant hand; feel love moving from the realm of your imagination to the realm of physicality as you do so. Look up at the moon, and at the first star you see, and say: *"Early light that guides the land, Seek and bring my love to hand."* ❤ TAKE A MOMENT HERE TO MEDITATE ON THE LOVE THAT YOU SEE ENTERING YOUR LIFE: consider the days to come when you will go somewhere you have always gone alone with a lover now holding your hand, and think of the light, airy feeling of having a special partner with whom to share your dreams, humors, and sadnesses. Touch the ribbon again to your brow. ❤ NOW LIGHT THE CANDLE AND DRAW THE MOON FULL INTO THE FLAME, asking it to dance there and celebrate your new, romantic life. As you work, ask the moon to bestow love upon you. Focus your thoughts from time to time by toasting the moon and your future success with a sip of the brewed sherry. Let the candle burn down about a third, then extinguish it with your ribboned hand (pinching the wick between your fingers, but being careful not to burn the ribbon). Repeat the ceremony for two more nights, until the candle is spent and the sherry depleted: before the next full moon your love should be by your side.

NOTE: *If you feel insecure about performing this spell at a tree in a public space—for instance if you do not have your own yard to work in—then by all means walk once to the tree, touch the ribbon to the tree when transferring it from brow to digit, and then return to the sanctity of your home for the candle burning itself. Try to make sure you can see the moon through an open window.*

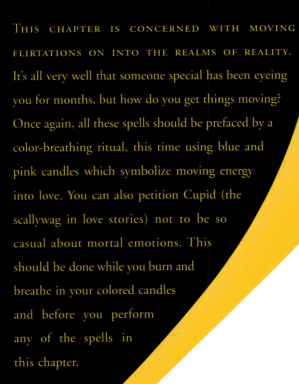

THIS CHAPTER IS CONCERNED WITH MOVING FLIRTATIONS ON INTO THE REALMS OF REALITY. It's all very well that someone special has been eyeing you for months, but how do you get things moving? Once again, all these spells should be prefaced by a color-breathing ritual, this time using blue and pink candles which symbolize moving energy into love. You can also petition Cupid (the scallywag in love stories) not to be so casual about mortal emotions. This should be done while you burn and breathe in your colored candles and before you perform any of the spells in this chapter.

The daisy wheel ♥ A SPELL TO TO OUST A CAD BUT PROVE AN ADMIRER'S SINCERITY.

YOU WILL NEED

A daisy; 2 dinner candles, in purest white; ylang-ylang oil; 2 dishes, each two-thirds filled with water

MOON PHASE: *Waxing, new to first quarter*

♥ AT ELEVEN O'CLOCK IN THE MORNING, PICK A DAISY AND MAKE A PRAYER TO THE GODDESS TO FAVOR YOU WITH TRUTH CONCERNING YOUR LOVE AFFAIR. Lay the daisy next to you while you work, notching your candles in seven equal places to make seven equal sections, then anointing each with ylang ylang oil, which is associated with honesty and revelations. Pull off the daisy petals and place them alternately in each of the dishes of water, saying the old rhyme *"He loves me, he loves me not"* as you work. Do not hurry. ♥ WHEN THE FLOWER IS DENUDED, light both candles and place one before each of the bowls, asking Venus to bring the "day's eye" to investigate the verity of your suitor. Ask for clarity about your lover with the words *"May the day's eye illuminate my hopes,"* and let the candles burn down the first notch. Repeat this each day for a week, during which time a true suitor will certainly reveal himself as such in deeds and words—whereas a bounder will retire.

Moonlit basil ♥ To MOVE A LOVE AFFAIR ALONG. This spell is suitable for a love affair that has already begun but appears to be going nowhere fast.

YOU WILL NEED

A basil seed; a silver container; a piece of paper on which you have written your loved one's name; a lock of his or her hair

MOON PHASE: *Last quarter*

♥ PLANT YOUR BASIL SEED IN THE SILVER DISH BY MOONLIGHT WITH THE NAME OF YOUR LOVED ONE AND THE HAIR UNDERNEATH. Tend it with love. The basil seedling will quickly sprout and flourish if there is hope of a good future together: by the time the first leaves appear, so will his or her advances if they are ever going to amount to anything.

Hair dressed, moon blessed ♥ THIS WAS MY GRANDMOTHER'S FAVORITE

LOVE SPELL. She had beautiful hair and wore the precious ornament through the many long years of her happy marriage to my grandfather.

YOU WILL NEED

A hair ornament of precious material, such as tortoiseshell, silver, or silk, or perhaps decorated with semiprecious stones

MOON PHASE: *Brand-new moon*

♥ CHOOSE YOUR HAIR ORNAMENT VERY CAREFULLY TO REFLECT YOUR PERSONAL TASTE AND STYLE. If you like, make it yourself from the raw materials above, which will personalize it all the more. You will need to wear the object often, so make sure it will be practical for you to do so. Before you wear your hair jewel for the first time, take it and bless it with the light of a brand-new moon. Hold it high with both your hands, surround it with beautiful ethereal light from the moon, and consciously imagine that light, which penetrates the mysteries of the night-time secret world and the dream world that we inhabit. See the moon kissing the pillow of the one you love; see the moon's face playing on your beloved's face that very night. Ask the moon to give you knowledge of your love's secret thoughts regarding you. Say: *"Beauteous moon, that shares my loved one's pillow, Surround him (her) with your protective halo, Reveal to me the course our love shall follow."* Kiss the object, then place it somewhere near where you sleep, but where it may catch the moon's rays for some of the night. ♥ WEAR THE CHAPLET EACH TIME YOU MEET YOUR HEART'S DESIRE, and matters will soon take off.

Das bandel ♥ ANOTHER BEAUTIFUL SPELL INCORPORATING RIBBONS. "Das Bandel" is old Viennese

dialect for a ribbon. Anna, an old friend from Vienna, exchanged this spell with me for the spell of my grandmother's (the one on the opposite page), and both of us were lucky in love.

YOU WILL NEED

3 x 30-inch lengths of ribbon, 1 fuschia pink, 1 rich scarlet red, 1 royal purple; a glass or cup from which your love has drunk

MOON PHASE: *Not important*

♥ THIS SPELL WAS TRADITIONALLY PERFORMED OVER A REST DAY, SO CHOOSE A SUNDAY OR, BEST OF ALL, A SPRING HOLIDAY. Cloister yourself away on your own for at least part of the day so that you can concentrate properly. Weave a beautiful braid from the ribbons, and as you weave, repeat the names of yourself and your beloved in sing-song fashion. When the braid is complete, lace the ribbons through your hair and around your head, and tie over your brow. (This may sound odd, but it can look charming if you add a few spring flowers and wear it in celebration of the season and the day.) You must keep the ribbons in your hair from sunrise till sunset—quite literally—and during the time you wear the chaplet send strong mental messages of love to the one who holds your heart. Drink water from his/her cup. Ask that the relationship move up a gear, that you may both declare your honest feelings and become more committed to one another (though not necessarily married). Contrive not to see your love at all during that day, but work hard on the telepathic messages. ♥ WHEN NEXT YOU SEE THE PERSON YOU WILL BE SURPRISED BY THE CONTENT OF THE CONVERSATION BETWEEN YOU; it will be as though you had telephoned to ask if you had any future together.

Waxing moon ❤ A SPELL TO INSPIRE HONESTY.

YOU WILL NEED

A tall, deep-blue candle; peony or lavender oil; parchment (or paper if unobtainable)

MOON PHASE: *Waxing*

❤ ON A WAXING MOON, ANOINT THE CANDLE WITH THE FRAGRANCE OF LAVENDER OR PEONY BY THE PUREST MOONLIGHT. By this same moonlight—and this light only—inscribe the name of your lover on parchment. Still by moonlight, use the name-paper as a taper to light the candle. Place the candle upon a fireproof surface, away from a window or curtain, and rest while the candle burns low. As you lay down your head that night, ask that your love be open and honest of his actions; ask that he leave off flirtation and reveal true feelings for you if he has them. Before a week has passed you will have a sign of his true regard.

"Out, out brief candle" ❤ USE THE POWER OF THE ELEMENTS FOR YOUR PURPOSE. This is a very theatrical spell to coax a coy lover to reveal a new or hitherto unseen part of his or her persona—but it will work only if there is a sense of destiny in the affair.

YOU WILL NEED

A photo of the one you love; a mirror (can be mounted on a wall); 6 small candles from the rainbow spectrum; a thunderstorm!

MOON PHASE: *Any*

❤ PERFORM THIS SPELL ON A WILD AND STORMY NIGHT AND USE THE ENERGY OF THE STORM TO COMMUNICATE YOUR SILENT MESSAGE TO YOUR LOVE. Place his/her likeness wherever it will be caught up in the reflection of the mirror, likewise the candles, so that when they are lit you have an eerie view of the loved one's face in the candlelight in the reflective glass. With all the force of the storm, urge his/her image to cast off any lethargy about the relationship with you, and commit more to it. Make sure that the candles continue to burn away as you address your beloved (I have known the wind put out several candles in relationships that have subsequently also petered out). If there is any passion in the pairing, your love will soon declare him/herself.

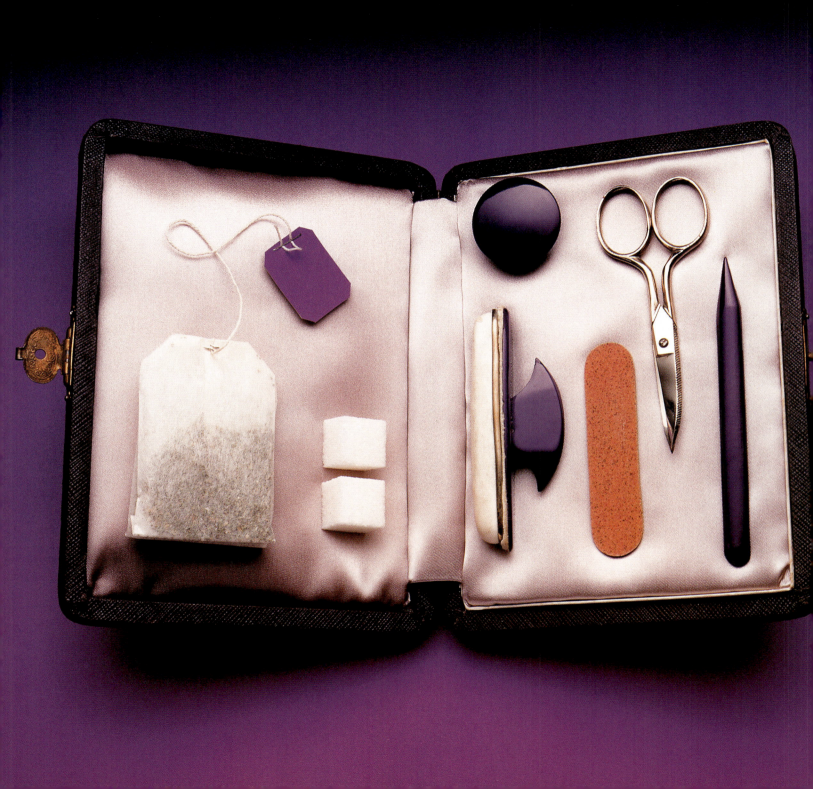

The manicure ❤ A LITTLE ADDITIVE TO HIS OR HER COFFEE BREAK.

YOU WILL NEED

Some nail filings from your recipient (not the dominant) hand; a cup of freshly made tea or coffee

MOON PHASE: *Any*

❤ WASH YOUR HANDS THOROUGHLY BEFORE YOU BEGIN. Chanting as you work, file your nails into his/her cup, saying the words *"Let me nail your true intent, Show me if your heart is sent, Straight to me without lament."* Add those little calorie-free filings without malice, and without trying to bind your love to you. The sipper will soon come forward if he or she is truly interested.

"Six flowers, six charms, six scented balms" ❤ ALSO

UTILIZING THE NUMBER SIX (THE NUMBER OF LOVE), the following spell employs lucky charms, flowers, and scents to map out the initials of the one you fancy. This is prepared at an altar of love, to nudge flirtatious affairs onto consummated ground.

YOU WILL NEED

Some pink velvet or silk; a pink candle; 6 flowers of any type, but pink in color; 6 small flower vases; 6 charms taken from the list on page 112, 6 drops of different aromatic oils of your choice, to anoint the objects

MOON PHASE: *Any*

❤ PREPARE YOUR ALTAR BY DRAPING THE FABRIC ACROSS IT, then burn a pink candle and address the goddess, asking for her help; do this for several days before performing the spell itself. ❤ PLACE THE FLOWERS IN THE VASES AND ANOINT THE CHARMS, then make the shape of your lover's initials by alternating vases and charms. Place the index finger of your dominant hand to your brow (beribboned in red or royal blue if you like), and concentrate on your question of fidelity or sincerity to your initialed love. Inhale the scents, and dab a little on yourself the next six times you see your love. On the seventh occasion passion will burst forth, or, if the designated love is a callous playboy/girl, the love affair will wither away.

The pansy offering ❤ IF SOMEONE YOU ARE STRONGLY ATTRACTED TO HAS BEEN

BUZZING AROUND YOU LIKE A BEE, going out with you on an irregular basis, or simply confusing you with signals of deep passion followed by indifference, this is the spell for you.

YOU WILL NEED

White or pink votive candles; 1 yard of purple ribbon and 1 yard of yellow ribbon; a photograph each of you and the person you love, approximately passport sized and with a clear likeness of the face; a yellow and purple pansy of the "face" variety (rather than plain colored; these usually have a tricolored effect and look like a little clownish face); a wooden bowl of water, scented with a few drops of either bergamot or clary sage oil

MOON PHASE: *Waxing*

❤ BEFORE YOU BEGIN THIS SPELL, TAKE THE TROUBLE TO DO A "CLEANSING REGIME" IN YOUR HOME: using a broom or a vacuum cleaner, physically sweep through the house, starting from the center and working toward the front door. Work up as much physical energy as possible. Now light the votive candles at strategic places in your home, saying: *"Blessings be to this place"* as you light each one. This should help to alter your outlook so that you become calm and serene. Wind the two ribbons around the index finger of your right hand, hold it to your forehead, and concentrate on the image of your love. ❤ NOW BREATHE THE COLORS OF THE PANSY, JUST AS YOU WOULD A CANDLE, AND PLACE IT BETWEEN PHOTOS OF YOU AND YOUR LOVER, with the photos facing in toward the flower. Hold the photos and pansy between your two hands for a moment as in prayer, and ask that honesty and fidelity visit your union. Talk to your love as though he or she were there: say what you would wish to say about not trampling your heart with indiscretions to others if his/her love for you is serious. Ask that if there is any possibility of a deep and lasting affection between you, he or she should by all means be playful, but stop playing games with your heart.

❤ NOW TAKE THE RIBBONS FROM YOUR FINGER AND WIND THEM TOGETHER AROUND THE PHOTOS AND PANSY, SANDWICHED TOGETHER. As you wind, say, *"If your love be true and dear, Make you your intentions clear."* Finish the sandwich with a tiny bow of both colours. Place the package beside or in front of the wooden dish filled with water. Put all the objects near an open window, somewhere they can remain undisturbed for seven days. Each time you pass the bowl, repeat the words of the spell. The following week the relationship will show its true direction.

Bound together ♥ Ribbons and cords have powerful magic work to do in revealing

and holding in place fragile growing feelings between new courting couples. I love this ribbon spell for its sheer playfulness and its "espionage" elements. It is, however, loving and harmless and draws on nothing sinister or worrying for your loved one. Perform it with humor, but in safety.

You will need

The tallest salmon-pink candle you can find; 1 yard of white or blue ribbon, ¼ inch wide

Moon phase: *Waxing*

♥ Take your candle and bind it with the ribbon, all the way from top to bottom, tying the ribbon into a pretty bow at the base. As you bind, say your loved one's name over and over, and ask your wish of Venus with the following words: *"I mean him (her) no harm, Bid him/her take no alarm, May our love be a balm, To heal and to calm."* Light the candle for a few minutes, being careful not to let the ribbon catch fire, repeating your prayer to Venus several times. Now extinguish the candle with laughter and warmth, unbind the ribbon, hold it across your open palms, and send a beam of love and cheerfulness to your beloved. ♥ The next piece of the spell requires a little inventiveness. You must take the ribbon to the one you like so much and carefully slip it into his (or her) pocket, or briefcase, or car. If you are discovered later, you can say it is a ribbon of protection, but try to get it there undetected. Almost miraculously, the relationship can move on to its next phase. **Sheronne and Robin have benefited from this lovely "ribbon dance." Each time he misbehaves, Sheronne pops a ribbon into Rob's lunchbox for work—sometimes tied around a Mars Bar. I know for a fact that he gets a lot more pleasure from this signal of her affection than he shows.**

Golden slumbers ♥ This spell has a long history in the Hardie family, and is held

in much affection by its younger branch. Like "Bound together," it employs an element of subterfuge, but it is failsafe in eliciting declarations of love and, often, some little luck with money as well.

You will need

A golden coin in current circulation; blue flowers, such as daisies, hyacinths, or bluebells

Moon phase: *Full*

♥ Place the golden coin between your palms and make a prayer (address whomever you feel comfortable with) for love to rise in a great wave and flood your life, and that of the person you love, with great happiness. Now take the coin and imagine your loved one's face thereon. Carry it to a circle that you have made from the blue flowers, and place it in the center of the ring. Leave it there on the night of the full moon, and in the morning take it to your love. You must contrive that he or she shall have it, perhaps to buy something on an errand for you. Once the coin (and it must be this very coin) has left your beloved's hands in a gesture of unselfishness, a display of deep affection will be forthcoming. In my experience this has always come before the next full moon.

Philip gave his coin to the lovely Lauren during the early days of their attraction. She in turn bought a scratch ticket in a small lottery with it. Enough money was gained to buy them both a wonderful dinner, and at this dinner their love affair moved onto an altogether higher plateau.

THREE'S A CROWD

3

"Two's company," the saying goes, but three has the dreaded reputation of causing havoc for loving couples. This may be because you cannot choose between two equally well-favored suitors, or it may be that the one you love cannot let go of the pain of a past relationship, unable to move forward to a loving future with you (or anyone else). This chapter is dedicated to the resolution of difficulties a third party causes; the magic that follows will help you to relegate the past to the past, exorcise skeletons from the love closet, or test the strength of your willing lover. . . .

♥ BEFORE PERFORMING ANY OF THE FOLLOWING SPELLS IT IS VERY IMPORTANT TO EXAMINE YOUR MOTIVES AND MAKE CERTAIN THAT YOU ARE NOT TRYING TO CAUSE HAVOC IN A CURRENT AND WORKING RELATIONSHIP. If you do not honor this code, the results will eventually be to your detriment. Remember, magic and the Wiccan path urge us to use the life force to attract and generate our own happiness—but not someone else's sadness! ♥ PREFACE EACH SPELL WITH A CANDLE-BURNING CEREMONY, cleansing the room and your thoughts of anything negative or sad; for this, breathe in the color pink of the love candle, and add amber, preferably by utilizing a piece of amber, to dispel the effects of the "crowding" of your relationship.

Bite the dust ♥ OR ACTUALLY, SAND! If your loved one shows every sign of being happy with you, but cannot quite let go of a past relationship, try this seaside ritual.

YOU WILL NEED

2 small pieces of high-quality flexible paper, such as parchment; a pair of nail clippers

MOON PHASE: *Waning*

♥ YOU MUST PERFORM THIS SPELL AT SUNDOWN ON A BEACH, EVEN IF THIS MEANS WAITING UNTIL YOUR VACATION. On one piece of paper write the name of the one you love; on the other, his or her love from the past. Make a little knot of the names, tying them together. Look at them in the palm of your hand, and say: *"I respect and understand that you have been that with each other which was tender and close; But if your love be truly over, Consign it to the past, And move on."* Now, bury the pieces of paper in the sand with the nail clippers and ask that affairs be manicured, trimmed, and tidied up. ♥ STAND NOW, BOW TO THE SETTING SUN, AND ASK BLESSINGS OF VENUS, WHOSE STAR WILL SHORTLY RISE. Ask that she may bestow on the other party a happy and a worthwhile love—in short, that he/she may find happiness elsewhere. Ask, too, that the past be now the past, and that the future belong to you. Kneel again on the sand and say: *"So mote it be."* ♥ YOU MUST NOW RELEASE YOUR OWN DOUBTS ABOUT THE PAST RELATIONSHIP. Regard the magic as already effective, and let no doubts haunt you from here on.

Amicable parting ❤ Like the previous spell, this will work only if you are

ridding your relationship of the last vestiges of a rival relationship that is, in effect, over. It is not appropriate for breaking up a viable marriage, real or in effect.

You will need

A photo of the couple who were together previously (this could be tricky but is very important; however, if you can't procure one, make a reasonable effort to interpret how they looked in some artwork of your own); some cupids with arrows cut out from cards, or something similar; a photo of you; a picture frame (optional)

Moon phase: *Waning*

❤ In this spell you make a new "tableau" of the way things will look when the past, spent relationship no longer has its negative binding power. Take the photo of the previous couple as the "heart" of your new collage, and place the cupids with their arrows pointing away from each other in opposite corners of the picture. Next to your love place your own photo, possibly trimmed into a heart shape so that the cupid nearest your love embraces you with his bow. ❤ At this point you may burn a candle and say a little prayer vouchsafing your good intentions as well as wishing luck and happiness on the third party (this is not part of the spell, but will "secure" it more if you choose to include it). Now you should create a "home" for this new picture—either in an album, or in a picture frame, or at a friend's house. Do make sure your loved one doesn't see it, for it will inevitably arouse a curiosity that will be difficult to satisfy.

The clover flower ❤ THIS SPELL IS AN ENTREATY THROUGH THE ASTRAL PLANE TO YOUR

LOVED ONE TO STOP TRIFLING WITH YOUR AFFECTIONS BY CONSTANTLY FLIRTING WITH OTHERS. A friend has suggested to me that it would be wonderful to do it en masse, to cure lots of people of both sexes of this irritating habit.

YOU WILL NEED

A clover flower, or, if this is not available, a leaf will do; a photo of the incurable flirt; a pink candle with a piece of amber placed in front of it

MOON PHASE: *Waning, preferably just after full moon*

❤ YOUR CLOVER FLOWER OR LEAF SHOULD BE PICKED ON THIS WANING MOON. Hold it in your hand and breathe upon it; hold the photo of the one you care for in the other palm and breathe on it too. Now light the candle, breathing the colors of the pink and the amber right into your lungs, heart, mind, and being. Surround your love in your imagination (and in the photo) with these same purifying colors. Addressing the candle, say to your love in your mind's eye: *"Do not trifle with my heart, May you from all others part."* Extinguish the candle, but repeat the process each day while the present moon continues to wane. If the magic is strong, and your lover essentially honest, other flirtations will soon cease.

Lawrence was a real Don Juan! Philippa had put up with as much as she could, but then put her pretty foot down. Now, she grows a clover plant at the back doorstep, keeps his photo in the whole patch, and lights a candle every waning moon. Result—the flirtations are now completely under control, and she smiles sagely as others try in vain to tempt her handsome partner into mischief.

❤ 53

The healed heart ❤ WHEN YOUR PARTNER HAS BEEN HURT IN LOVE MORE TIMES THAN YOU CAN COUNT AND HAS LOST ALL HEART FOR A SECURE FUTURE, employ "heartsease" to turn the tide of his or her luck.

YOU WILL NEED

A plain blue or creamy white pansy (one color only, save for the "eye"); some beautiful (perhaps handmade) paper, pink, oat, or white in color; some calligraphy pens; a picture of the loved one, or a lock of his or her hair; a pinch of ground orris root; a white or blue candle to match the flower

MOON PHASE: *Full*

❤ YOU MUST BEGIN THIS SPELL BY PRESSING THE PANSY (HEARTSEASE) TO YOUR BOSOM. Imagine it quickly cleansing away the pain, then infusing color and hope into your beloved's heart. Keep the pansy and, before the next full moon, make a pansy mandala. Draw a wheel on your paper, placing the pansy and the picture of your lover or lock of his/her hair right in the center. Secure it with a little glue and sprinkle orris root over it. Now, around the flowery center, carefully write a prayer to release your loved one from past pains. Use your own words, but make sure they are a sincere and unselfish reflection of your wish to see the person happier—hopefully with you. Include the full name and birthdate of your loved one, and the words *"Amor vincit omnia"* ("Love conquers all"). Finally, cover your mandala with some tissue paper, and place it for safekeeping in an envelope or plastic sleeve. ❤ ON THE NIGHT OF THE NEXT FULL MOON, TAKE THE PRECIOUS MANDALA TO A CANDLE WHICH YOU LIGHT WITH THESE SAME WORDS, *"Amor vincit omnia,"* then pass the mandala through the candlelight. Imagine your love free from darkness and loneliness, shedding the confusion and sadness of times past. Finally, place the mandala in a safe place, such as a photo album, with a picture of your love, or with a letter or card received from him/her. Keep it always.

Letting go ♥ The pansy, or heartsease, rules again in this next spell, this time creating

a ring of protection and power to drive off unlucky or unhealthy love. You could use violets instead, for these have many properties in common with the pansy.

You will need

Some hard apple cider (buy a commercial cider if you wish, but infuse it with extra power by adding fresh apple rings); an oak cleansing bath (described fully in my previous book, Hocus Pocus, *but essentially a bath into which acorns and oak leaves have been put as a purifying ritual); a ring about 1 yard in circumference of pansies or violets*

Moon phase: *Last quarter*

♥ Drink your cider in the cleansing bath, imagining all cares washing from your body. Feel the warmth of the bath penetrating your very essence, and think of this as an omen of new warmth in a future life. Toast the moon and the goddess with your cider, and when you have finished your bath, tip a little cider into the roots of an oak or other tree near your house, offering a libation to the wood spirits who may cleanse your world. Finally, sit in the midst of the fairy flower ring and pray for new growth in the one special relationship you wish to move forward. Sit long enough to be honest about past errors, and be clear about your intentions for future happiness. Pledge also to spread this new-found happiness among your friends.

♥ This spell works wonders if you cannot let go of a past love affair yourself.

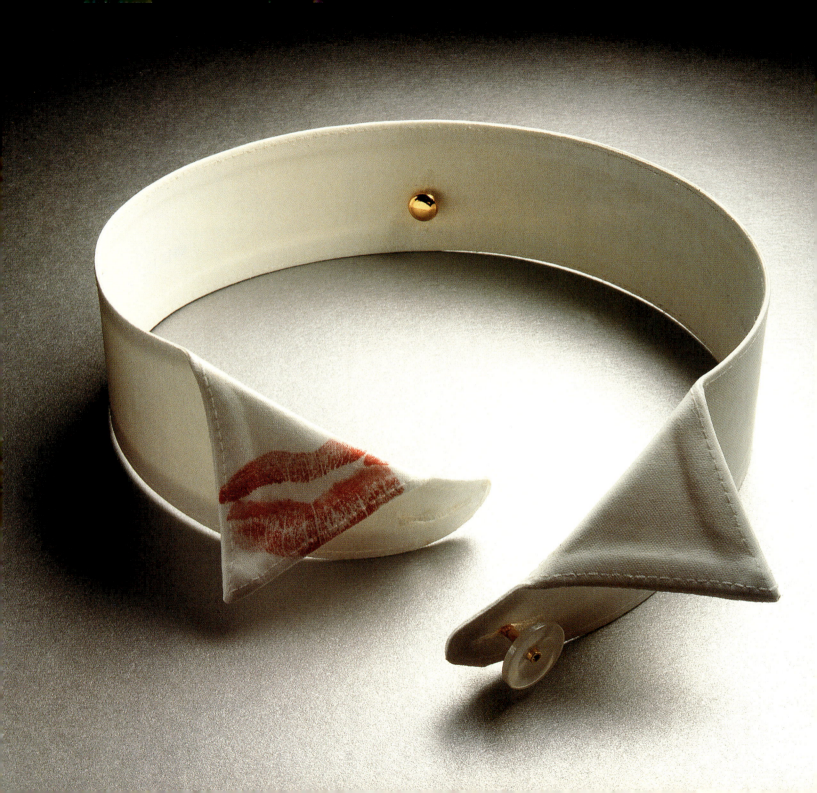

Icy calm ♥ NOT EVERYONE IS SCRUPULOUS IN THEIR APPROACH TO FINDING A LOVER, citing the saying

"All's fair in love and war" to excuse their conduct when head-hunting a love who is in truth already committed. Sometimes the relationship bearing the brunt of the attack is strongly in need of an overhaul, but often it is just the act of a determined flirt wreaking havoc for the sake of a gratified ego. If someone is poaching in your forest, defend yourself by freezing them out.

YOU WILL NEED

Paper with the name of your rival written upon it; an ice cube tray; symbols, as below

MOON PHASE: *Last day or two of the old moon*

♥ FREEZE THE NAME OF THE INTRUDER IN AN ICE CUBE TRAY ALONG WITH A SPECIALLY CHOSEN PAIR OF SYMBOLS: one, chosen from the appendix, to represent your love, and the other something like a key, or an acorn, to unlock the enticing quality this third party seems to have over your partner. Utter the following incantation: *"With your attentions be not hasty; My love, and you, shall soon be frosty; Drink of another if you be thirsty; Another's kiss you'll find more tasty."* This is a humorous spell, but it leaves in no doubt the fact that you are saying *"Hands off"*! A change will quickly occur.

The lock in honey ♥ IF YOUR LOVE HAD A TERRIBLE CHILDHOOD and is insecure about

making attachments, try this second freezer spell.

YOU WILL NEED

A lock of your lover's hair; a lock of your hair; a small padlock; a tiny freezer-proof container; some honey; an early snowdrop or bluebell

MOON PHASE: *Any*

♥ WEAVE THE LOCKS OF HAIR TOGETHER (SECURING THEM WITH THREAD IF NECESSARY), place them together in a padlock, and then into the freezer container. Pour honey over the top like a healing balm, asking that it sweeten all memories of past sadness; then place the flower head into the honey. Secure the container, put it into the freezer, and blow it a kiss as you close the door. At regular intervals, blow the charm a kiss. This spell can produce amazing results if done with strength and sincerity.

Three candles bright ♥ THE IDEAL CHOICE IF THE OTHER PARTY CAUSING TROUBLE

IS NOT NECESSARILY A PAST LOVER, but perhaps an over-possessive child from a previous relationship, or an in-law (my husband calls them "outlaws").

YOU WILL NEED

3 candles, colors chosen from the rainbow spectrum to represent the 3 different parties (such as star sign or birthday number colors)

MOON PHASE: *Any*

♥ NOTCH THE CANDLES IN SIX EQUAL PLACES (TO BURN THE CANDLES DOWN OVER SIX NIGHTS), AND WHEN THEY ARE ALIGHT, say aloud the name of your "adversary," adding: *"Let go your immaturity and fear, Let [name of the loved one] find love's security right here."* Touch your heart as you say this, and wish the other person well. Repeat this over the next five days, and you will find his/her possessiveness gradually lessens.

The beech leaf spell ♥ IF BOTH YOU AND YOUR LOVED ONE HAVE BEEN BRUISED IN

LOVE TOO OFTEN, perform this spell at the first sign of difficulty between you.

YOU WILL NEED

A beech leaf, picked on a warm day; a book of value, such as a missal, diary, or volume of love poetry

MOON PHASE: *Any*

♥ HOLD THE BEECH LEAF TO YOUR HEART AND ASK THAT IT CLEANSE YOU AND GIVE YOU NEW SPIRIT. Taking it from your heart, secretly stroke it over your love's brow (contrive a little tickle or gesture of affection), silently urging it to cleanse away negativity and fear. Smile at your love, then place the leaf reverently into the chosen book. Sleep on this for a month, and the love between you will wax. (This spell also works well if you have been having trouble deciding that a past love affair is truly over.)

Cast adrift ♥ PERHAPS THE LOVE AFFAIR YOU HAVE WITH YOUR OTHERWISE PERFECT MATE IS BEING HINDERED BY THE "PRESENCE" OF A PAST LOVE WHO IS MORE APPEALING THROUGH ABSENCE. If the specter of a previous lover haunts your happiness, here's how to turn the tide.

YOU WILL NEED

2 little handmade boats, such as a child would make from paper or cardboard, but strong enough to be, if not seaworthy, then at least riverworthy; paints and markers to decorate the boats; a photo or drawing of your partner with his or her previous love

MOON PHASE: *Full (tides high)*

♥ THE MORE CARE YOU PUT INTO THE DESIGN AND EXECUTION OF THESE BOATS, THE MORE POWERFUL WILL BE YOUR MAGIC WORKING. One boat should be named after your love and the other after his/her past lover, painted or carefully marked so as to be reasonably waterproof. Place an object belonging to your loved one in his/her boat, and something belonging to your rival (if you have such a thing) in hers or his. Using a picture of the erstwhile couple, make a little flag, cut it in half, and glue one half to each boat. Lastly, to the boat named for your love, add your name in the form of another flag. ♥ ON THE FULL MOON, TAKE YOUR BOATS TO THE WATER'S EDGE AND KNEEL. Praying for happiness for all the parties named, ask that the past love release your love and allow everyone to move on with their lives. Make sure to wish your rival happiness in a new life. Now launch the boats, facing them away from one another. Watch for a while to see if they set sail in opposite directions. Urge the elements to separate them if this is just. After a short space you will know if you have any hope of seeing them go their different ways. If your boat sails well, your hopes should soon be riding the crest of a new wave.

Shirley has performed this spell on many occasions for her man, for his past memories and pain are deep. However, she is tremendously kind, patient, and persistent, and has secured more happiness with him than any of her previous rivals. They battle along on the high seas, and no one deserves greater happiness—which will yet come in full measure.

4

THIS CHAPTER IS WRITTEN FOR THOSE LOVERS WHO ARE THROUGH PLAYING GAMES. It's wonderful that you've had a nice strong relationship for the past however-many years, but your mind is, not unnaturally, skipping on to weddings, or children, or whatever your dream may be. So, if you're ready for that commitment, and it seems to have been too long in coming, perhaps it's time for a little magical intervention. Preface each of the following spells with a candle cleansing/breathing regime employing a blue/indigo candle. Relax totally, gather your courage internally, concentrate your thoughts, then unleash a little enchantment.

Bright white light ♥ Preparation for marital magic is a serious business.

In addition to the color breathing just described, it is recommended that you perform this first spell in tandem with any other spell from this chapter. It is like making proper homemade pastry for a magnificent pie—so please don't omit this.

You will need

A photo of you and your lover together; 4 blue/indigo votive candles and 4 white

Moon phase: *Any*

♥ Start by concentrating your thought forces on the photo. Generate energy from your fingertips and toes, and imagine a great white light starting from you and filling the room, encircling the photograph as it gains power. Through the white light, tell your loved one what a formidable couple you are, and how much stronger you would be together in the world if united. Send the idea of your union lots of love: surround the "couple" with light and power. Now place the photo in the midst of the candles, which should form a ring, alternating indigo and white. Light them clockwise, and swirl your love around your partner.

Love adorned

You will need

A tarot card representing Arcanum VI, "The Lovers"; 2 different-colored ribbons, each 1 yard long; a needle with large eye; a beautiful box padded with feathers (like a nesting box)

Moon phase: *First quarter*

♥ Choose the colors of the ribbons to represent you and your love (choose your favorite colors if you like). Lovingly embroider the tarot card however you wish with the ribbons. As you work, imagine embroidering your relationship with sunshine, light, color, and love. Make sure that the colors interweave, and tie the ends securely in a small knot. Now write your names, preferably in calligraphy (intricately interwoven if you like), around the card. Place the tarot card in a box softened with feathers, and send it a final blast of vibrant light before "putting it to bed." Cherish it. Proposals will follow.

Pressing your suit ♥ A TASTY TRICK TO WIN OVER YOUR LOVER. Ginger is a spice whose

properties have long been prized. In medieval times, there was a tradition of making ginger cakes and cookies, often in the shape of a playing card, and decorating them with gold leaf for feasts and fairs on holy days. The hearts suit was the popular choice, the ace being an invitation to love. The two might indicate a marriage proposal. The other cards in the suit were sometimes picked by young girls "blind" as a kind of divination—getting the king or the knave meant you would meet someone special at the fair itself. If you want to make one of these beautiful treats and keep it for yourself for luck in love, choose the nine, but if you want to give one to your love to excite his or her senses or to progress the love affair, the ace must be your choice.

YOU WILL NEED

Your favorite recipe for ginger cookies, or gingerbread, to which you should add 1 or 2 drops cassia food oil; 1 sheet of edible gold leaf for decorating

MOON PHASE: *Any*

♥ MAKE YOUR RECIPE WITH THE CASSIA ADDED. While the gingerbread or cookies are still warm, add the gold leaf in the decorative pattern of your choice, following the manufacturer's instructions.

NOTE: *Edible gold leaf can be ordered from New York Cake and Baking Distributors: (800) 942-2539.*

The walnut shell ♥ SINCE ROMAN TIMES, WALNUTS HAVE BEEN SYMBOLS OF NUPTIAL

BLISS. This is largely because within the shell the nut divides perfectly into two entities; but also, nuts are symbols of fertility and a high-protein food. The lovely spell that follows is possibly an adaptation from Roman times, and looks forward to the walnuts' being used to make the "marriage bread" (wedding cake).

YOU WILL NEED

About 12 walnuts, whole in their shells; a pouch made up of 4 colors of velvet, to your own design if possible; a drawing or photograph of you together as a couple; a blossomed bower, traditionally strewn with petals of orange blossom, but rose or another fruit blossom is also suitable

MOON PHASE: *Not important, though you must perform this spell in spring*

♥ USING THE WALNUTS, TRACE THE INITIALS OF YOUR BELOVED'S NAME UNDER A TREE OR IN A QUIET CORNER OF THE PLACE WHERE YOU LIVE. Lay your hands over the letters/walnuts and infuse as much love and strength as you can into them. Imagine scenes of children dancing, a May dance, you and others bedecked with flowers and ribbons—in short, a marriage ceremony. Let the initials stand while you sew up your velvet pouch, which must be big enough to contain all the nuts. When you have finished, put the photo of both of you into the pouch, then put the walnuts on top. Close the bag with a ribbon or drawstring and carry it in procession to your "bower." (If you live in the city, make your bower in a corner of your apartment by creating a leafy haven and strewing the area with your chosen petals; do not disturb it once you have created it.) ♥ THE POUCH MUST NOW PASS THIRTY DAYS IN THE BOWER, and each day around 11:00 a.m. and 3:00 p.m., hold your palms toward it and close your eyes for a moment. The spell is "closed" by placing the pouch in a coat or a bag, or a treasure box, and sweeping (please, no vacuming) the petals out of the house or bower. They must be returned to earth, so toss them on the ground. ♥ WITHIN THIRTY DAYS TO THIRTY WEEKS (LESS THAN THE TWELVEMONTH) THE BUSINESS OF YOUR MARRIAGE WILL BE DISCUSSED. **Gabriele and Deborah have a garden full of blossoming trees, and a beechwood bowl of walnuts forever in their house, in deference to this spell.**

The springtime shower ♥ THIS SPELL HAS MUCH IN COMMON WITH THE

PREVIOUS RITUAL, drawing on the powerful scent of orange blossom, which in the East has long been connected with marriage. Again, the petals and a photo are used, but in this case there is a candlelight vigil. Although this may be slower to work than some spells, it is nevertheless very powerful and a pleasure to perform.

YOU WILL NEED

A photo of the happy couple you wish to be or, better yet, a sketch; a ring to lay atop the picture; a small piece of cord; a white dinner candle anointed with neroli oil; orange blossom petals (Philadelphus, or mock-oranges will do if you can't find the real thing); orange blossom oil (neroli)

MOON PHASE: *Start near full*

♥ ON A WINDOWSILL OR A SMALL TABLE, LAY THE PICTURE AND THE RING, AND PLACE THE CANDLE BEHIND THEM. Every day for seven days, shower the picture with petals and a verbal message of love (your own words). Dab on the oil (dilute it if necessary if you have sensitive skin) and wear it each time you see your love, and for the seven days of the petal shower.

♥ AT THE END OF THE WEEK, ROLL THE PICTURE INTO A SCROLL, TIE IT WITH THE CORD, AND LIGHT THE CANDLE. Put on the ring and wear it now until the magic is completed. You must keep a candle lit on your "love altar" for as long as it takes to get the offer you await. One couple I know keep their wedding picture on an altar with a candle and orange blossom, just to be sure!

The silken kerchief ❤ This spell also uses the powerful associative symbolism

OF THE RING AND AN ALTAR, and it, too, takes many days to unfold.

You will need

A silk handkerchief; embroidery thread; a golden ring, though not necessarily a valuable one; a love altar (similar to the one described opposite)

Moon phase: *Brand new moon*

❤ Your skills with a needle are required here, so take your time embroidering the whole name (middle as well) of your beloved onto the handkerchief in beautiful coloured threads. Use quite dominant colours so that it reads clearly. Now, embroider your own name by weaving it in and out of the letters as artistically as you can, using related but paler colors. As you embroider, sing a love song and send sweet loving thoughts—but nothing too heavy. Be confident that you are making great progress with little steps, and do not be impatient. ❤ When the embroidery is finished, pass the kerchief through the ring saying: *"The love we have is a gentle force, To others it brings amity; For we two may there now be unity."* Tie the kerchief into a knot with the ring and place it on your altar, or in another place you deem sacred. Let it lie for thirty days (the moon's duration) and await some occurrence.

The red candle ♥ Also for a Friday, this spell uses red, the color of action, to get an

inert romance moving toward the altar.

You will need

A lock of your lover's hair; a bowl of the herb yarrow; a red votive candle; any piece of jewelry given you by your loved one

Moon phase: *Brand new*

♥ On the chosen Friday of a new moon, place a lock of your love's hair into a bowl of yarrow, which is an extremely potent magical herb with a very soothing fragrance. Bow your head and ask for earnest love; ask that if this relationship be not destined for growth and future happiness, that it reveal itself thus, allowing you to find a suitable partner with whom to settle.

♥ Now light the votive candle and pass the jewel through the space above the flame. Repeat: *"Amor gignit amorem."* Let the candle burn down, often repeating these words, and keep candle, bowl, jewel, hair, and yarrow in proximity to each other for a month. Thereafter things will improve one way or another.

The brooch ♥ A brooch set with the loved one's hair was a trusted amulet and

keepsake in Victorian times. If you can find a jeweler to work with you on this, it makes powerful magic.

You will need

A lock of your lover's hair; a lock of your own hair; a specially made locket or brooch

Moon phase: *Not important, but the jeweler's work should begin on a Friday*

♥ Weave the strands of hair into a beautiful love knot. Sometimes they look effective made into an intertwined pair of initials. Take your prize to a jeweler, who should set them into a specially made locket or brooch, preferably covered with glass. When you receive the brooch back, take it to the moon of the first night, and the sun of the following day, and ask: *"Enlighten our lives; May our nights share ever after the hours of the moon, and our days the hours of the sun; May our two lives, and our two souls, now be as one."* Within three months you should be setting a date.

The red cabbage ❤ This extraordinary vegetable produces a beautiful "star" when

cut across. It is a sacred place to treasure up the names of two people who love each other, for they will prosper together.

You will need

A small red cabbage; the names and photographs of you and your beloved

Moon phase: *Full*

❤ Cut through the cabbage to reveal the "star" in its heart. Place the names and pictures of the two of you into the cabbage, and replace the halves, saying: *"[Name], Love me little and love me long, that we may grow together strong."* Secure the cabbage with foil or plastic wrap, and take it to the full moon, where, holding it high, you repeat the rhyme. Now put it away for safety in the fridge for a week, then transfer it to the ground. Soon you will have your proposal of marriage, if ever you are to have it with this person.

Charmed! ❤ A peaceful spell. Perform it when gentle rain is falling.

You will need

2 charms, chosen to represent you and your partner (see page 112); water taken from a running source, such as a stream, collected on a new moon; a jar or other small container

Moon phase: *New*

❤ Anoint the charms that represent you and your heart's desire with water you have collected from a running source by moonlight. This can best be accomplished by retaining the charms in a small jar or other vessel filled with the water. Say the following over the charms: *"Marriage in heaven is surely made, Let our hopes and amity never fade."* Think about the words and make a promise to yourself never to become complacent about the union you now so desire. Undertake to keep it and cherish and feed it: do not make this vow lightheartedly. Now the charms should be removed, and the water, on this rainy day or evening, thrown back into another running source. Once again, make a plea for the fulfillment of your desires, but do not renegne, once you have your wish, on the pledge you made to acquire it.

The myrtle mantle ♥ MYRTLE WAS A FAVORITE OF THE VICTORIANS AND WAS USED IN QUEEN ELIZABETH II'S WEDDING BOUQUET; but its pedigree as a love talisman is older, for the Greeks and Romans thought it the property of Aphrodite (Venus). Winners at the original Olympic games wore it—and so should you if you would gain your prize.

YOU WILL NEED

Some myrtle flowers and leaves; a coat worn by your love, and one of your own; some boughs of myrtle for an altar; 7 small lavender-scented candles (one for each day of the week)

MOON PHASE: *Any*

♥ SEW SOME LEAVES AND FLOWERS INTO THE POCKETS OF YOUR FAVORITE COAT, AND, WHILE FEIGNING SOME REPAIRS, SEW SOME INTO THE POCKET OF YOUR PARTNER'S. It can be a well-loved jacket or an overcoat, and the addition need not be very bulky. Now prepare an altar of myrtle, laying a fresh cloth and placing boughs of the plant across it; amid the greenery place a candle, lavender scented or anointed with lavender oil. Light the candle at moonrise, saying: *"Better we wed over the myrtle than over the moor."* (Better to marry the one you know than a stranger!) Wish for married peace and harmony. Let the candle burn awhile. ♥ EVERY NIGHT OF THE WEEK, REPLACE THE CANDLE WITH A FRESH ONE, repeat the words, and stroke the leaves of the plant to release its fragrance. A proposal must surely follow.

POTENT WITH PASSION

THERE'S SOMETHING HERE FOR ALL OF US! The spells that follow are dedicated to anyone who would put a little more passion into their relationship. Many of these spells, which include love potions and aphrodisiacs, were created originally for fertility, as an absence of libido limited family numbers, but for many this will prove the most popular chapter, as all the spells are fun to perform and have quite a range of applications. Preface all spells with a little color breathing (purple or wisteria); when candle burning, anoint with rosemary oils for men, or with melissa (lemon balm) for girls.

The silken cord ♥ LOVE ENTWINED. This first spell has a long history: my grandmother used to describe it as "ancient," and seeing its classical symbolism I think it may have come to Britain with the Romans.

YOU WILL NEED

A strand of your loved-one's hair and a strand of your own; some embroidery thread in three different colors of your own choice from the spectrum on page 11; 3 x 1 yard lengths of silken cord in colors to match the thread; some "Cupid's tears" oil: 2–3 drops each tuberose, jasmine, and ylang-ylang oil and 1 drop musk oil blended with 2½ teaspoons almond oil

MOON PHASE: *Full*

♥ MAKE A "GIRDLE OF VENUS" FROM THE INGREDIENTS AS FOLLOWS. On the full moon, weave together the strands of your and your lover's hair and wrap them in three colors of embroidery thread, securing all the ends in a knot. Now braid the cords, and as you work, sing your love a song of love—any that makes you think of him or her by association. Weave the words of the song in with your girdle. In the center of the girdle loop the hair and thread braid around the braided cords, then secure the ends with anything decorative you like: tassels are probably best, but you might choose charms or shells or anything that feels personal and satisfying. The girdle is complete, and you should wear it for the first time with the oil dabbed between breasts, behind knees or earlobes, etc., on a night that will undoubtedly witness unbridled passion. The magic of the girdle empowers the wearer, and the scents excite the nose that receives them.

My girlfriend Georgia wears her girdle to smart corporate dinners as well as for alfresco dinners in the garden. She seems to have Barry (her sexy but much older husband of many years) well and truly where she wants him—happy and mischievous with her alone.

Red ribbon # 3 ❤ A SPELL FOR GIRLS TO DRIVE THEIR PARTNERS WILD.

YOU WILL NEED

1 yard of red ribbon; a few drops of Cupid's tears oil made from 2–3 drops each tuberose, jasmine, and ylang-ylang oil and 1 drop musk oil blended with 2½ teaspoons almond oil; a beautiful thigh-high stocking; tiny votive candles in rainbow colors to line the path to the bedroom

MOON PHASE: *Any*

❤ AFTER FIRST SPRINKLING THE RIBBON WITH A LITTLE OF THE OIL, TIE IT AROUND THE TOP OF YOUR STOCKINGED THIGH. Make the following incantation to Aphrodite: *"May I now recall the way I claimed my love's heart; May I show him the palace of love incarnate; Allow his cares to lighten and smilingly play his part. So mote it be."* You must have the ribbon and stocking in place and seduce him with all your charms this night (no matter how hard his day at work or problems with partners and children and in-laws and cars). Light the way to the boudoir with the candles, and make this a romantic and passionate night to eclipse all others. ❤ HEREAFTER, WHENEVER YOU CAN, PLACE THE RIBBON IN ODD PLACES FOR YOUR MAN TO FIND: in his address book, his wallet, his briefcase, his pocket, around his coffee cup in the office (contrive this how you will). Each time he sees it, it will make him long to be with you.

My sexy friend Fiona sent a courier to her man's car; using her spare key the courier "broke in" and tied the ribbon around his steering wheel just before close of play for the day at his office. She also had the courier tie the stocking around the gearshift, and I understand he nearly drove off the road in his eagerness to get to her.

Pheromone-a-therapy ♥ A spell for the boys. This works on similar lines to the one on page 84, but you can use a commercial fragrance to the same effect.

You will need

A blend of oils of your own choice including citrus smells (bergamot, lemon, grapefruit, etc.) or a brand-new aftershave

or scent—something you have never worn before, tried from a wide range and selected for a clean, citrus type of smell,

or an oceanic fragrance if you prefer

Moon phase: *Any*

♥ You must woo her as in days of old: Cook something special, light a path to the bedroom door with candles, leave the kids with a neighbor, buy beautiful new linen for the bed and put it on beforehand—anything to change the usual routine at home. Contrive to make passionate love to the lady, and use your new fragrance for this first occasion. Use it sparingly, and take as much trouble to create a special ambiance as you can. ♥ Thereafter, spray the scent sparingly on various items when she least expects it: her business cards; her scarf; her pen; her umbrella; perhaps in her handbag. Used humorously, it will drive her crazy with desire.

The lavender candle # 2 ♥ To make him burn with desire. You will learn

much in magic about the power of the lavender candle. Ideally, this should be a candle already scented with lavender oil, but if this is not available, you can make your own by steeping a lavender-colored candle in lavender flowers and essential oil in an airtight jar (such as a pasta or flour jar) for at least two weeks.

You will need

1 dinner candle of absolute lavender color infused with scent in the above way; a needle or sharp implement for writing in the wax; a magnet

Moon phase: *Waxing*

♥ Working by moonlight, alone, if possible, notch your candle equally in fourteen places, with seven notches on one side of the candle and the other seven placed alternately on the opposite side. On the front and back of the candle, soften the wax by leaving it on a warm surface; warm the implement with which to write, then inscribe your name or initials on one side and your lover's on the other. Place the magnet in front of the candle and, after color breathing the color wisteria, light your candle. ♥ Vividly send powerful, sensual messages of passion and lovemaking to your partner as the candle burns; hold onto the magnet as you do so. Send thoughts of love and warmth also, not just physical passion, lest you upset the balance of true feeling you have for each other and make the affair purely physical. Repeat the procedure at the same time each night while the moon waxes, and you should find the passion aspect of your love relationship quite renewed from the moment you begin. It may be helpful to keep the magnet in the bedroom (or wherever else the opportunity for lovemaking may seize you) from now on.

The strawberry and starflower cup ♥ THE FIRST OF TWO

SURE-FIRE LOVE POTIONS. Beautiful heart-shaped strawberries have always been associated with indulgence of the senses and a luxury of love. Wild strawberries, which were originally used in many potions and herbal treatments, have a wonderful fragrance and are high in iron and potassium, both of which instill strength and courage. This perhaps explains their wide use in love potions. When combined with sparkling alcoholic drinks (or soda water for teetotalers), their properties enter the bloodstream faster, and in combination with viper's bugloss (a relative of borage) or borage itself (sometimes called starflower) can induce the required gentle mood of euphoria.

YOU WILL NEED

1 teaspoon young viper's bugloss leaves, or borage leaves and flowers (if you can't get borage or bugloss dried or fresh, use a few drops of starflower oil, which is widely available); 1 teaspoon sugar; 1 tablebspoon fresh or 1 teaspoon dried wild strawberry leaves; about 1 dozen cultivated, or 2 dozen wild, strawberries, halved (wild have stronger properties and fragrance); a squeeze of lemon juice; a bottle of sparkling wine; a charm, chosen from the appendix to symbolize your lover and frozen into an ice cube

MOON PHASE: *Full moon*

♥ SPRINKLE THE HERB LEAVES/FLOWERS AND STRAWBERRIES WITH THE SUGAR AND A LITTLE LEMON JUICE (OR ADD THE OIL) AND ALLOW TO STEEP FOR ABOUT HALF AN HOUR IN A SMALL DISH. Add about one small glass of the sparkling wine to the mixture, and leave to infuse for another two hours. During the preparation process, concentrate your thoughts of desire on the one you love, and send warm and loving thoughts to him or her as you work. (For added power, tie a lavender-colored length of ribbon around the index finger of your right hand as you do this.) Finally, skim the leaves from the liquid, leaving the strawberries, and add the concentrate to the remaining sparkling wine. Pour into a glass, and add the ice cube with the special charm frozen inside (a silver heart or golden arrow is traditional). This aphrodisiac potion will inject great passion into your relationship.

The secret of cognac ❤ FROM FRANCE, ANOTHER POWERFUL POTION DEMONSTRATES

THE EASE WITH WHICH YOU CAN EXCITE PASSION just by varying a simple sip of brandy.

YOU WILL NEED

A small flask of good cognac or armagnac; oranges and lemons, sliced, and orange and lemon flowers if available; borage flowers; a silken stocking

MOON PHASE: *Full*

❤ ALLOW THE COGNAC TO STEEP WITH SLICES OF LEMON AND ORANGE AT ROOM TEMPERATURE FOR TWO OR THREE HOURS, then add the borage flowers and steep for another two hours. Strain the liquid through a silken stocking and say: *"Je voudrai l'amour de [name]; c'est l'amour qui fait le monde la ronde."* ("I desire the love of—; it is love that makes the world go round"). Sip the potion in low light with your beloved. You will be surprised how much it warms the blood and fires the passions.

Viola odorata ❤ TO MOVE YOUR PHYSICAL RELATIONSHIP TO DIZZYING NEW HEIGHTS. Violets

were the food of passion created by Jupiter to feed his beloved Viola (Ione). The Greeks used violets to perfume confectionery, and it was an important component in Roman love potions. Violet wine was declared a potent inducement for lovers, and it also cured hangovers. Take, then, a leaf from their plants and mix some violet wine.

YOU WILL NEED

2½ teaspoons violet flowers, fresh if possible (it is worth growing the plant in a pot and harvesting the flowers when sweetest and most strongly scented); a bottle of dry white or mellow red wine; some slices of kiwi fruit if using white wine, or plums if red.

MOON PHASE: *Any*

❤ MAKE AN INFUSION OF THE FLOWERS IN THE WINE BY SOAKING THEM IN THE CHILLED RED OR WHITE FOR THREE DAYS. The wine should now be very gently warmed in a pan (not boiled), then cooled again. Strain the flowers out, add the sliced fruit, and serve with apparent insouciance. You will soon find your partner working overtime to excite your attentions.

Top ten aphrodisiacs

♥ GREEN TEA IS NOW SAID TO BE A CURE FOR MANY ILLS, but of old it was an ingredient to strengthen and excite the humors of the body. Make a pot and sip throughout the day.

♥ LAVENDER EXCITES! Use it sparingly as a culinary tease of taste buds and senses: "Pasta Lavandula" is included in the last chapter, but lavender can also be added to a number of sauces with interesting effects. My own favorite is to make a Lavender Hollandaise, incorporating a few drops of lavender oil, or some fresh flower buds, into the yolks as you begin to beat them. You may never need dessert. . . ♥ ANOTHER DYNAMITE CONCOCTION IS PARSLEY AND CILANTRO PESTO, made by blending a large handful of flat-leafed parsley, the same of cilantro (in both cases the fresher the better), and 2 cloves of garlic with 2 tablespoons olive oil in a food processor. This is strong stuff: Gabriel and Patricia, who use it regularly, can't dismiss their Sunday dinner guests quickly enough once the effect cuts in. ♥ I HAVE A FRIEND WHO IS EVERY INCH THE COURTESAN: what secrets of love does she not know? She is convinced that the best cure for frigidity is a warm bath—what I might now call "Eike's antifreeze." Her secret ingredient is melissa (lemon balm) oil, which should be added to a bath as it is running with a small amount of salt and some almond oil. This simple solution cures, soothes, and delights the female body; if lemon balm tea is sipped simultaneously, the result is an insatiable appetite for pleasure! ♥ MEN HAVE A SECRET RECIPE, TOO: rosemary is an excellent tonic for those suffering nervous disorders, anxiety, or stress; so a bath with rosemary oil added could go a long way to heal his "headache" the next time he claims he has one, and you have other ideas. ♥ OYSTERS ARE SO FAMOUS IN THIS CONNECTION THAT IT WOULD BE CHURLISH NOT TO INCLUDE THEM. What they do have going for them is a sensational texture, and they also give the consumer lots of strength. ♥ IF THE OBSTACLE TO PHYSICAL LOVE IS ONE OF NERVES ON BOTH SIDES, champagne must be recommended, even without the potions added to it in these pages. It enters the bloodstream faster than ordinary wines and has a cheering effect for most people. Take it as an aperitif with oysters, and let the double-whammy effect send you both into the stratosphere. ♥ A SENSUAL MASSAGE WITH APHRODISIAC OILS WILL PUT ANYONE IN THE MOOD FOR LOVE: but the best for passion are undoubtedly lemon grass, jasmine, ylang-ylang, and, best of all, tuberose, exotic and erotic beyond belief (so long as budget is not a problem). ♥ HONEY WAS SO RENOWNED FOR ITS APHRODISIAC PROPERTIES THAT IT GAVE ITS NAME—"HONEYMOON"—to the month of newlywed passion. It can be used in a variety of delicious ways as an aphrodisiac—perhaps taking a tip from the Polynesians, who annoint their vital parts with it for a stimulant, lubricant effect.

♥ POPPY SEEDS ARE ESPECIALLY GOOD FOR ADDING ZING TO SEXUAL PERFORMANCE. Athletes who have eaten poppy seed rolls apparently give positive results for drug testing, so sprinkle them liberally.

Heartsease and honey ♥

FOR ONE WHO HAS BEEN THROUGH A DEMANDING OR SOUL-DESTROYING RELATIONSHIP WITH A LOVER WHO HAS COST HIM OR HER DEAR IN CONFIDENCE, the following brew may help to heal the heart, body, and soul. The wild pansy, or heartsease, has numerous other common names, reminding us of its former status as a love charm and ingredient in love magic: kiss-her-in-the-buttery, loves-lies-bleeding, cuddle-me. Use it in this brew, which makes a good wintry alternative to the earlier, more summery potions.

YOU WILL NEED

No more than ½ cup dried heartsease (especially flowers, but some leaves); a bottle of red wine; a pinch each of nutmeg, cloves, and cinnamon; 1 teaspoon honey; candles to burn during sipping, in colors echoing the tricolor of the flower

MOON PHASE: *Any*

♥ LEAVE THE FLOWERS AND LEAVES TO SOAK IN SOME COOL RED WINE FOR ABOUT AN HOUR. Add the spices and honey and let them infuse for another hour. (Be careful not to make the brew any stronger as it might otherwise cause nausea—the opposite effect to the one desired!) Heat the wine gently for ten minutes, then strain the liquid into warmed cups. This must be drunk hot, by candlelight, and is excellent if enjoyed in a bath big enough for two.

This wine is very addictive in its own right. Even if there is nothing whatsoever the matter with your relationship, try this recipe anyway to enjoy the delicious effects of sharing it with a loved one.

Carnations, nuts, and ruby wine ♥ To enhance a lackluster

sexual relationship. Unlike the other love potions, this brew requires a little magic ritual for its making. According to magic belief, the ritual and the words will transform the properties of the carnations which are at the center of this spell.

You will need

10 scented pinks (Dianthus caryophyllus)*; a bottle of red wine; lettuce leaves; some whole nuts, including hazelnuts, walnuts, almonds, and pecans*

Moon phase: *Waxing*

♥ First perform your color-breathing ritual with lighted candles, then make a ring of the flowers and sit in their midst, facing east. Send a mental message to the one you love, whose physical presence you crave, and with whom you have a less than perfect sexual bond. Look in turn at every carnation flower, and see your love's face therein. Inhale the perfume from each bloom, sending a mental message of its fragrance to your love. Breathe in the color and fragrance from the flowers, and then begin circling your head (very much as you would in a relaxation exercise) from the base of the neck. Be sure to work clockwise, for if you work "widdershins," or counter-clockwise, your love affair will go backward and "unwind." Close your eyes and say: *"Scents and sense are for our ease; Now our sensual love moves to a heightened phase."* ♥ Take the flowers and denude them of their petals, but very lovingly. Retain half in a plastic bag in the fridge for the salad, macerate the petals of the remaining flowers in the wine, then leave the mixture somewhere cool for eight days. Heat the liquid gently (never boil) and repeat the words over your "cauldron" (or whatever pot you are using to brew the wine). Strain and thus recover the ruby color of the wine; it should now be perfumed with the fragrant carnations. ♥ On the night you wish to sip the brew with your beloved, make a green salad with any leaves you like, plus the nuts, and the petals of the remaining carnations. Dress lightly with oil and vinegar. (If you have time, add some clove carnations to the vinegar for a few days to intensify the flavor.) This should now form a first course—or with luck maybe the only course—to dinner. If your love affair had previously lacked a little lust, this should do the trick. Repeat whenever necessary.

6

THIS FINAL CHAPTER ADDRESSES THE CHALLENGE OF KEEPING LOVE FRESH IN LONG-TERM RELATIONSHIPS—if you like, extending the honeymoon period through the years. By realizing the need to do this, we are halfway to beating the "banality blues." Here we employ playful magic, simple ways to inject romance into everyday matters which constitute the reality of life with your partner. Recognizing the realistic probability of rifts, we look at new ways of making up, too. Preface all your magic-working with the now familiar ritual of color breathing; the color for perfect love is true rose pink, and your scent options this time are lemon or rose.

The magical note ❤ MUSICIANS ARE REGARDED ASTROLOGICALLY AS THE "CHILDREN OF

VENUS," AND SHAKESPEARE DESCRIBES MUSIC AS THE VERY "FOOD OF LOVE." Most of us have a song or piece that relates beyond anything else to the person we love. Music is fundamental to the workings of this next spell.

YOU WILL NEED

Some blank business cards, for your own special message; as many candles, votive size, as you have words in your song (see below); a few drops each of carnation, sandalwood, and frankincense oils; a musical note in the form of a charm, vase, or picture

MOON PHASE: *Any*

❤ FOR THIS SPELL, WHICH SENDS SIMPLE AND CLEAR MESSAGES OF LOVE MAGICALLY AND HYPNOTICALLY TO YOUR PARTNER, you need to settle on a few words of your own choice to pour into your lover's soul. Either choose some music that relates to your partner, such as a favorite song or piece you play or sing together, or speak from the heart and use your own imagination. In any case, choose words that are uplifting but unburdensome: *"I will always love you"* would be a good choice, but *"I can't live without you"* has connotations that are too heavy. ❤ WRITE EACH WORD ON A CARD, and place each card under a votive candle. Blend the oils and anoint yourself and the candles. Hold the music charm in your hand, and sit in the center of the candles, thinking vividly of the sight, sound, and smell of your beloved. Breathe in his/her presence as if it were real. ❤ Now START THE MUSIC, AND LIGHT THE CANDLES IN THE SEQUENCE OF WORD ORDER. Imagine you are looking right into your loved one's eyes and dwell on some physical feature you like, such as a dimple, a curl, or a mole. Dwell on each and every word in turn, very slowly, one word at a time, as though you were trying to send just that word to your love's consciousness. Don't hurry. Smell the oils, which add concentration and clairvoyant ability, and continue to see the face, laugh, smile that you love through each word transference. ❤ MAINTAIN THE THOUGHTS LONG ENOUGH TO CONVEY THE WORDS OF THE WHOLE PHRASE, then imagine you are sending all the words and candlelight and smells through the air to your partner. Send laughter and a smile of your own by way of a "lots of love" at the end of your message; then release all together. Extinguish the candles one by one, and treasure the charm until you can give it to your love. You will shortly see a tangible sign of the spell's subconscious message at work. Your relationship will quite perceptibly become that little bit stronger.

The love rainbow ♥ MY HUSBAND AND I PRACTICE THIS SPELL EVERY YEAR ON THE

ANNIVERSARY OF OUR MEETING, always using flowers from the beautiful garden he has created for me from a bare patch of land.

YOU WILL NEED

6 x 1 yard lengths of ribbon, 6 flowers, and 6 votive candles in matching colors, chosen from the list to suit your own numbers,

but making sure to include rose pink (perfect love) as one of the six

MOON PHASE: *Any*

♥ ON THE MOST IMPORTANT DATE OF YOUR RELATIONSHIP (such as first meeting, engagement, or wedding), place a candle encircled with a matching ribbon at its base, and a flower of matching color, in every room in the house. If you have a small apartment, place all the colors in different areas instead. Choose purple or wisteria color (and flower if possible) for the bedroom, and rose pink for the room that most represents the "heart" of your home: this might be the kitchen or living room, the dining room, or even the garden if you love this best and entertain or sit there together most contentedly. ♥ ONCE YOU HAVE PLACED THE ITEMS, take your partner by the hand and walk through the house, lighting each candle as you go. As you do so, swirl the color from the candle around the room, and in so doing, imagine you are freeing yourselves from all negativity and indolence in the relationship. Finally, stand together holding hands—the witch's symbol of marriage—and swirl the color and peace around each other. Embrace. ♥ NOW YOU ARE READY TO FACE ANY TEST, AND YOUR LOVE WILL CONQUER ALL. At the end of the spell, gather together the flowers and make one bunch of them in the place where the rose pink candle burns. Here it should remain, in a vase, for seven days.

An elemental love ❤

EARTH, AIR, FIRE, AND WATER. One of the most important rituals in magic is the recognition and honoring of the elements that make up our world. This beautiful and complex ritual would make an excellent alternative wedding ceremony for anyone reluctant to have a civil marriage.

YOU WILL NEED

2 varieties of pink flower in 2 different pink hues (a pale pink and a deeper pink rose would be ideal)—you will need enough flowers to yield 50–100 petals; a pink candle for the altar; pink fabric; some benzoin incense; a velvet bag or wooden bowl; 4 locations for scattering the petals, including running water or the sea and, most significantly, a hot-air balloon

MOON PHASE: *Full*

❤ HARVEST OR BUY YOUR FLOWERS TOGETHER FOUR DAYS BEFORE THE MOON IS FULL. Pluck off the petals you have each chosen to represent the other, then present them to your partner. Working together, create a love altar from the pink fabric and candle, cleansing the area first in your mind. Working with your partner's petals, make out his/her first name, tracing the shape of each letter with the petals; ask that he/she do the same with yours. Ideally, the two names should interlace. Now light the candle and incense and, holding hands, ask blessings on your relationship. Address whomever you please, but think of the true divine spirit. Ask that love's alchemy work to bring a new attainment and wisdom to your bond. ❤ ALLOW THE ALTAR TO STAND WITH THE PETALED NAMES FOR FOUR DAYS, lighting the candle for a couple of hours each day/evening. ❤ ON THE DAY OF THE FULL MOON, PLACE THE PETALS IN A VELVET BAG OR A WOODEN DISH AND TAKE THEM TO EACH OF THE ELEMENTS SAVE AIR: begin by scattering some petals over the earth in a much-loved place, saying: *"We are of the earth made, and our love grounded in fertile warmth."* Thence to the sea, or a river, where you should cast some of the petals into the water, saying: *"We are of water made, and our love flows together like streams meeting, gaining strength and consequence in the union."* Your next stop is to a fire, symbol of passion, indoors or outside. Spread some of the petals over the wood or into the coals, saying: *"Our love speaks the language of passion, it warms and transforms our senses, it glows like the power of the sun, and our strength is forged anew in flame."*

❤ AT SUNSET, TAKE THE REMAINING PETALS EITHER TO A HIGH AND HOLY PLACE, or, for sheer exhilaration, take a hot air balloon ride; from the air or your high place, say, lastly: *"Our love is also spirit, vital as the air we breathe, powerful as the wind in a storm, gentle as the breeze which caresses your cheek and teases your hair. We are in all elements, one."* Strew the petals as you fly. Your names are now at one with heaven and earth, and you are bonded lovers for all eternity.

The constellation ♥ A SPELL TO PLACE YOUR LOVE AFFAIR IN THE HEAVENLY REALM.

You need to use your decorating skills to create your own beautiful firmament with deep blue background and golden stars to form a celestial canopy above the "marriage bed."

YOU WILL NEED

Some paint suitable to decorate the ceiling in evening-sky blue; some gold leaf, or good-quality gold paint; blue candles

MOON PHASE: *Any*

♥ THE BEAUTY OF THIS SYMBOLIC RITUAL IS TWOFOLD, in that you are creating a signature piece of artwork to bless your chamber, which should be aesthetically uplifting; at the same time, the concept is to lie together under a microcosm of the heavens in which your own individual beings are given special significance. The effect is to exalt your love. ♥ SET TO WORK PAINTING THE SPACE ABOVE YOUR BED IN THE BLUE YOU FEEL HAPPY WITH. Take time, and do not rush the job just to finish it, for the more effort you put into perfecting the decoration, the more you will be aware of the time it takes for a relationship to grow to full beauty. Once your backdrop is finished and dry, begin the magic of the task: using your gold paint, create a galaxy of stars, the overall aim of which is to subtly spell out your and your love's initials, or names, or even symbols that act for each of you, by intertwining the stars across the night sky. Burn candles as you work, infused with incense or just of a plain color that suits your mood. Pour love into your design, and think what concept of a divine love you can aspire to, and recognize. Play gentle music while you work if it pleases you—in short, do anything that helps to imbue the project with a peaceful, loving status under which your physical, earthly love can thrive. ♥ REMEMBER THAT, AS WITH ALL MAGIC, this requires a level of mental focus and peaceful concentration; it is the thought forces that create the magic, and the physical work merely symbolizes your ideas, giving them a solid and tangible existence. ♥ WHEN FIRST YOU LIE WITH YOUR PARTNER UNDER THIS CANOPY, preferably by candlelight, concentrate together on the effect of the "starlight," and make a pledge together always to seek to put your bond and life path onto the highest possible footing—walking in the stars.

The key talisman or three locks ♥ THE SYMBOLISM OF LOCKS AND

KEYS, AND THEIR MAGICAL STATUS, occurs frequently in the tradition of witchcraft. To begin with, there is an obvious sexual connotation in lock-and-key; and then, too, there is the sense that the one grants, and the other denies, access to something precious or private. A superstition persists, in many country places that to drop—and especially to break—a key is unlucky, and suggests moving away. Here, though, the locks and keys are seen as something hopeful and propitious, the sharing of knowledge between two people and the subsequent intimacy that this brings.

YOU WILL NEED

2 keys cut for your front door, or for each of your cars, or for some other private and appropriate place; a lock of your partner's hair and one of yours

MOON PHASE: *New*

♥ DECIDE WHICH PAIR OF KEYS YOU ARE TO USE, BASED ON A SENSE OF WHERE YOU AND YOUR LOVE ARE MOST "AT HOME." Your key might be that of a diary or letter drawer, his perhaps his car if he travels in it all the time; otherwise, the house you share together is the obvious choice. ♥ ON A NEW MOON, take the keys to a jeweler who can have them plated in silver or gold for you; or, better yet, have the keys made in silver if they are small enough. While the keys are worked on, or straight afterward, have both sets of your initials engraved on them. If this takes some days, wait for the next new moon before performing the next stage of the spell. ♥ TAKE YOUR KEYS AND GO TOGETHER TO A SET OF CANAL LOCKS, then bless them with an incantation of love of your own choosing: this symbolizes the steady journey into extended parts of your world, and is, of course, concerned with water, the element of emotion. On the same day, go together to a green place (a garden or park is perfect) and cut a lock of each other's hair, which should then be passed through the loop at the top of the key. Place both the lock of hair and the key together in your pocket, or a matchbox, or somewhere they can remain together while you make the return journey to bless the keys at their final place, the locks they fit. Say something here along the lines of: *"Abroad or at home, give us strength and intimacy together; May we unlock each other's hidden selves, and thus grow better aware of what we are together. Each object has individual merit, strength and meaning: but together, they reveal something precious and treasured."* ♥ NOW, EACH OF YOU SHOULD PERMANENTLY CARRY THE OTHER KEY, aware that certain arcane elements of each other's personalities may now mysteriously and subtly come to light. You must pledge in your hearts never to abuse these precious insights.

Honeyed rose ❤ This is another beautiful embodiment of entwined love, which has the added bonus of curing quarrels and past strife.

You will need

2 pieces of paper about 3 x 1¼ inches; a tiny jar; some honey; a beautiful rose bush, traditionally a two-colored variety such as Rosa mundi, or R. Ferdinand Pichard

Moon phase: *Any*

❤ Write your name on one of the two pieces of paper and your partner's on the other and, kissing them, tie them into a knot together. Put them together in the little jar and cover with honey, then replace the lid. Now, plant your rose, together if possible, but you can do it alone if circumstances so dictate. Say something like: *"We are earthly creatures, living here on this earth, which is sweetened by the gifts of nature's bounty, and by the knowledge for each of us, of the other's existence. May we make of our earthly selves the most that we can, and joining together, sweeten and beautify our own and our friends' existences."* Water, cherish, and love your rose. Cut blooms from it regularly to place at your love altar. Every year, place a new "knot" in the soil under its roots, and restate your love and intent.

Pasta lavandula ♥

TO CALM THE MIND AND EXCITE THE SENSES. This pasta dinner involves performing a spell before the arrival of the loved one, then throwing together a dinner *à deux* based on lavender and its oil, which have the properties to soothe and calm while at the same time exciting the senses—ideal for preserving the perfect love. Quite literally, it injects the unexpected into the everyday.

YOU WILL NEED

6 x 1 yard lengths of lavender-colored ribbon, of varying lavender hues if desired; 1 bunch of lavender; 6 small lavender-scented candles; a small photo of you and your loved one together, smiling or laughing; ribbons of pasta prepared with a light dressing of olive oil, salt, and lavender flowers; a salad containing flowers

MOON PHASE: *Full moon*

♥ BEGIN BY WINDING THE SIX RIBBONS LOOSELY AROUND YOUR RIGHT HAND (or left, if you're left-handed), and keep them there while you work. ♥ PLACE THE BUNCH OF LAVENDER IN A VASE IN THE CENTER OF THE TABLE WITH A RING OF CANDLES AROUND IT, then set the table with the place settings opposite one another. ♥ PASS THE PHOTOGRAPH ACROSS THE LAVENDER FLOWERS IN THE TABLE BOUQUET. Light the candles, pass the photograph over the flame of each one, then lay the photo in the middle of the ring of candles and imagine sending your partner a strong electric current of love in the shape of a beam of lavender-colored light. It will help you to do this if you touch the ribbons to the center of your forehead. Hold the vision of your loved one in the light for a few moments, then relax, unwind the ribbons from your hand, extinguish each candle gently, and encircle each candle with one of the ribbons. ♥ LEAVE THE TABLE EXACTLY LIKE THIS WHILE YOU PREPARE THE DINNER. Mix the lavender flowers, olive oil, and salt together and set aside. Prepare the salad. Cook the pasta, and, just before you're ready to eat, add the lavender dressing; infuse all your love into the plate, and place it before your lover. Ask him/her to relight the candles (still with the ribbons encircling them), and wait to see what transpires at the end of the meal. **This spell is extremely effective if both partners are exhausted from everyday life and need help getting the romance and passion back into their relationship.**

The glass of Venus ♥ A MIRROR HAS A POWERFUL CONNECTION WITH VENUS AND

HER HANDMAIDENS, as does the shell from which she was born. Honor these two potent symbols of love, and she will honor your union.

YOU WILL NEED

A small piece of mirror glass, cut to a size that will sit happily somewhere in your bedroom; a strong frame for the mirror; shells of many sizes; gold paint (if desired)

MOON PHASE: *Any and many*

♥ THIS IS A WORK OF MAGIC THAT MAY, REALISTICALLY, TAKE MANY MONTHS TO UNFOLD. The symbology is beautiful, and the resulting glass will be a constant reminder of the reflection of your love for one another. Begin by having the mirror framed (you can buy one framed if you find one you truly like), then set aside a table or work area for the long process ahead. Together with your partner, if possible, work the shells around the mirror's framed edge, gluing them in place as artistically as possible. Combine sizes and shapes; work together on one patch, or start from opposite corners. Sing or talk sweetly to one another while you work; play music you both enjoy. Employ the consciousness precipitated by the candles of your color choice. Work little and long rather than in haste; and never quarrel in front of your mirror. Remember, this is a very special piece you are working on, and should reflect the best of your love for each other. ♥ WHEN YOU HAVE FINISHED SETTING ALL THE SHELLS IN THEIR PLACE, you may wish to gild the edges with gold paint or leave them natural to suit your taste. The resulting glass will be beautiful and should hang or stand in your bedroom. **This spell can be applied in numerous ways: one close friend of mine worked on her glass while her love was away in another country. On his return, she gave him the glass, and their relationship has gone from strength to strength ever since.**

Appendix ♥ FOR MAGIC TO WORK PROPERLY, IT MUST CONTAIN AN ELEMENT OF INDIVIDUALISM, FOR

IT IS A PIECE OF YOURSELF, YOUR OWN PSYCHE OR SOUL, THAT YOU ARE GIVING TO THE WORKING. The best way to do this is to add one symbolic charm, or perhaps just a plain object that you identify with the person you love, and/or with yourself. This might range from a straightforward representation, such as a rebus (picture-word) revolving around your beloved's name (an arrow, say, for a "Fletcher," a piece of metal for a "Smith," etc.), an object he or she loves, (a musical note for a musician or music lover, a boat for a traveler or sailing enthusiast), or, best of all, a more mystical symbol which you alone understand. The following is a selection of symbols that have a long association with magic ritual. Choose freely.

ACORN: growth from small beginnings; also fertility and divine protection.

ANGELS AND CHERUBS, OR PUTTI: messengers of the gods and, in antiquity, harbingers of love.

APPLE: sacred to Venus / Aphrodite; it has a star when cut across the middle. A golden apple signifies persistence.

ARROW: attribute of Cupid: in gold it kindles love, but in baser metal it spurns love.

BASKET: of flowers, signifies hope; of fruit, fertility and passion.

BAT: symbol of the passing night, and the witching hour.

BEE: hard work. Also humility in love, and the healing of hurt, recalling Cupid being stung by a bee while stealing a honeycomb. A beehive is a blessing of love on your home, a place where sweet honey will grow. A very lucky charm.

BELL: to claim somebody's attention.

BIRD: symbolic of the soul. A goldfinch is said to have acquired its red spot swooping to pluck a thorn from Christ's brow on his path to Calvary; an owl is wise; a European blackbird is especially magical, as its song enchants the listener; a dove is the bird of Venus.

BOAR: signifies passion untamed.

BOAT: someone who travels, or is abroad.

BOOK: symbolic of someone learned; also knowledge itself.

BOW: a hunter, or the same attribute as Cupid's arrow.

BUTTERFLY: reincarnation and, specific to love, gentleness.

CAMEL: ability to endure time apart from a loved one.

CANDLE: many symbolic references to light and knowledge and, in love, the kindling of the spark into a steady flame.

CARDS: according to individual divination. The ace of hearts: an invitation to love; the nine of hearts: a wish fulfilled; a king or queen: represents the loved one; a knave: not to be trusted.

CARNATION OR PINK: a symbol of betrothal, especially if red.

CAT: lucky for witches; they know the secrets of the night.

CHERRY: the fruit of paradise.

CLOVER: always lucky, as cattle fed on it were seen to thrive; a four-leaf clover is especially lucky.

CORN: fertility. Also, a sign of some special news.

CRUCIBLE: a symbol of alchemy.

DICE: a gamble.

DOLPHIN: these creatures drew the chariot of Venus; hence, they bring love.

DRAGON, DRAGONFLY: fertility and power; also the symbol of anything Welsh!

FATHER TIME: he unveils truth, and shows that, in the end, right must prevail.

FLOWERS: from Flora, the bringer of spring and, thus hope and renewal.

FOUNTAIN: Representative of the garden of love.

FROG: privy to the secrets of witchcraft, a lucky emblem.

GLOBE: someone who has lived in more than one country, or the desire to travel.

HARE: sometimes a witch, a messenger, or possibly a timid person.

HONEY: in a pot, or as a comb, symbol of strength and sweetness in love.

IVY: immortality, as an evergreen, thus tenacity in love and all ventures.

KEY: fidelity in love.

KNOT: symbol of an indissoluble union. The strongest is in a figure-eight.

LADDER: ascent, or upward progress.

LADYBUG: very lucky symbol of providence in the home, and a good omen for travel.

LAUREL: in a wreath, the prize of knowledge; also, excellence.

LILY: purity and devotion; a tiger lily is passionate love.

LOOM: symbol of the woman weaving, and so, enchanting.

LYRE: suggestive of poetry, and the ability to woo. Where Orpheus laid his lyre, violets arose.

MIRROR: self-knowledge, and truth.

MOON: lamp of the night. Central to most magic-working, and love divination; connected with the ebb and flow of emotions.

MORTAR AND PESTLE: the magician or alchemist.

MOUNTAIN: something of enormous size, or foreign.

MUSICAL INSTRUMENTS: symbols of love, as musicians were regarded as the children of Venus.

MYRTLE: a powerful talisman for fidelity in marriage.

OAK: the tree of strength and wisdom, most sacred to the Druids. Love will conquer.

PANSY OR HEARTSEASE: the most potent flower for love.

POPPY: symbol of hypnotic power, sleep, and dreams.

QUINCE: from Venus, a powerful fertility fruit and symbol of marriage.

RABBIT: strongly connected with Venus and, of course, fecundity.

RAINBOW: an arc of communication with the gods, personified by Iris in classical mythology. Very strong in magic, since the blending of all the colors makes the perfect white. Recreating the rainbow spectrum around your dwelling ensures good fortune.

RIBBON: see Thread.

RING: Universal symbol of eternal love and authority.

ROSE: flower of the Virgin and, especially, the bloom of love, since it is sacred to Venus: legend tells that at her birth, roses suddenly appeared. The pricks from its thorns are likened to the wounds of love. Originally the white rose was sacred to love, but when Venus hastened to help the dying Adonis, a thorn pricked her foot and stained the rose red with her blood. Thus, the red rose is a symbol of passion.

SAIL: also sacred to Venus, signifying her birth. Used often to symbolize a traveler.

SEAHORSE: an extremely fortunate symbol, the messenger adapted for sea and land, beloved of the gods.

SHELL: especially scallop or nautilus. Symbol of foreigners, and especially strong in love, as it is sacred to the birth of Venus. Also powerful for blessings of the home, since it is itself a home to sea creatures.

STAG: usually a personal emblem, known for fleetness and sharp senses which help it to avoid capture. It is connected with the sense of hearing, and its stillness is aspired to by practitioners of magic.

STARS: literally, divinities: to speak to a star is to converse with the gods themselves.

STORK: the bringer of news, connected with Mercury.

SUNFLOWER AND, SOMETIMES, MARIGOLD: Flower of ardent love turned forever to the Sun; used in magic to disperse gloom.

SWAN: sacred to Venus, and thus, lovers, because swans drew her sea-chariot.

SWORD: an emblem of justice. Sometimes, in love, it represents a tortured soul.

THIMBLE: a powerful charm, symbol of patient work. Can also signify anyone who works with his or her hands.

THREAD: usually woven into three, symbolizing the Three Fates. In magic this transmutes to a ribbon.

TRIDENT: emblem of the sea, and of Neptune. Sometimes chosen by a Piscean as his or her personal charm.

UNICORN: most magical of all animals, and protector of women. Allays poison. People who see unicorns can see fairies.

VINE: the harvest, most significant part of the calendar in magic.

VIOLET: humility and sweetness; a necklace of violets protects from deception, and it is sometimes regarded as the flower of Cupid. Violets sprang up to feed Io when she was changed by Jupiter into a heifer to protect her from Juno's jealousy. Thus, they are the food of love.

VIOLIN OR VIOLA: A specific to the "music of the spheres," thus, beguiling love.

WAND: symbol of knowledge, and directed thought. The talisman of the magician.

WEB: symbol of spinning and spiders, and thought to be very lucky. Spiders often help humans who have shown warmth and regard for living creatures. The web is connected with the "web of life" and the strands of human destiny.

WHEAT: plenty, like corn.

WIND: either Zephyr, the warm west wind, which, as husband of Flora, brings the flowers of Spring; or Boreas, the cold wind from the North, which terminates affairs of the heart, or signifies a long period of endurance.

WINGS: Victory of the spirit.

YARROW: the witch's herb and, properly, a nosegay for a new bride.

Essential oils in magic ♥ In my grandmother's day, many of the fragrant

BREWS SHE USED IN SPELLMAKING WERE UNSIGHTLY, TO SAY THE LEAST. The properties of the herbs and their essences, however, were crucial to the psychological state of the spellmaker, and unpleasant orors sometimes had to be endured. Not so today, when aromatherapy has made little bottles of essential oils familiar to all. The short list here is only a précis of the oils most usually used, or those that have a multiplicity of functions. Use them according to instructions for room fragrancing, candle anointing, and bathing.

BASIL: a good all-round oil, focuses the mind and cheers the spirits.

BERGAMOT: helps combat introversion and downward mood spirals.

CAMOMILE: excellent when you're worried or tired.

CAMPHOR: a good telepathy oil; also used to disenchant unwanted admirers.

CLARY SAGE: restarts your flat battery.

CYPRESS: sometimes used to calm anxiety and jealousy.

EUCALYPTUS: cuts through the ether; a good clairvoyant oil.

FENNEL: curbs appetite.

FRANKINCENSE: a prince of oils; excellent for leveling emotions and allaying fears.

GRAPEFRUIT: traditional for detaching someone from the past.

HYSSOP: mainly for money and prosperity.

JASMINE: very sensual; expensive, but a lover's scent and helps to overcome sexual apprehension.

JUNIPER: often used in protection rites and general love spells.

LAVENDER: useful for everything: passion, purification, insecurity, protection. Also invaluable in the first aid box for treating burns, bites, and skin complaints.

LEMON: deals with selfish thoughts.

LEMON VERBENA: traditional scent for love messages.

LETTUCE: sleep-inducing, calms overly strong sexual appetite.

LEMONGRASS: stimulates the system; good for someone who shows lack of interest in love

MANDRAKE: for use on altars only. As famous as Macbeth; the strongest magic herb.

MARIGOLD: telepathic and nurtures love.

MARJORAM: calms hostility and anxiety, thus good for reunion dinners.

MELISSA (LEMON BALM): a female herb; also good for treating fright and shock.

MEADOWSWEET: may not be available as oil, but strew the herb on altars. Very cheering.

MYRRH: for talking to the divinity.

NEROLI AND ORANGE: a marriage oil.

ORRIS: if not available as oil, use powdered root. All love matters.

PATCHOULI: brightens the mind, improves creative energies.

PEONY: (perfume oil) very exotic; also good for money spells.

PEPPERMINT: the right oil to use for studying and focusing thoughts.

ROSE GERANIUM: like lavender—a thousand purposes! Erotic; creates, and breaks, attachments, so useful in many spells.

ROSE ATTAR: pure rose oil: the most valuable in love spells. Also soothes nerves and counteracts sadness or grief, and can level thoughts that are too strongly nostalgic.

ROSEMARY: a male scent. For clarity of mind, and a bringer of action.

SANDALWOOD: a good love oil: deals with feelings of self doubt and lingers in the imagination; also very purifying.

VANILLA: exotic. Used in love charms and potpourris.

TEA TREE: the Australian answer to lavender; sets healing in process.

VIOLET: wash hands and bathe head with this or rose (diluted in warm water) before performing love spells for a really powerful current in your magic.

YLANG YLANG: the third crucial sensual oil; counteracts anger and frustration.

The tree/moon calendar of the Druids ♥ THE MONTHS

OF THE YEAR WERE MARKED OUT BY THE CELTS IN THE THIRTEEN MOONS, which they named after the sacred trees. Each moon was measured from full, that being the greatest power, to full, and the first moon of the year was that falling closest to Yule (December 21). They also have connotations that might help your magic. ♥ THE MOON MONTHS ARE: Birch, or less usually, olive: roughly late Dec.–Jan.: the moon of beginning; rowan: the travel moon; ash: the healing moon, ruling tides; alder: spirit moon, concerned with self-guidance; willow: the moon of love and fertility, the real witch's moon; hawthorn: the peace moon; oak: approximately mid-year: the strongest moon; holly: the moon to disenchant, moon of prophecy; hazel: the wise moon, moon of actuality; vine: moon of the harvest; ivy: the moon of protection and partnership; reed: the domestic moon, moon of motherhood; elder (sometimes myrtle): the moon of completion, moon of banishment. ♥ SOME MAGIC WAS WORKED OVER THE COURSE OF THE WHOLE YEAR BETWEEN THE BIRCH AND ELDER TREES. You may wish to enhance your magic by incorporating a branch or some wood from the relevant tree in your spell according to the time when you are performing it.

Index

AUTHOR'S ACKNOWLEDGMENTS:
Biggest thanks in the world for the existence of this book go to Zephyrine Losey, b. August 14 1996, who magically ensured the success of its predecessor and makes my life a joy; and Joe Johnson, born in the same week as Zephy, baby son of the talented Michael, who with David Jones at Johnson Banks delivers this volume to all in this beautiful state of aesthetic grace. Less esoteric thank-you's are due to the indefatiguable Anne P, the most encouraging friend and editor; Fiona Mac, who has worked with real love and dedication; Sara, for her extraordinary still-life photos of absolute magic; Samantha, my baby witch; my grandmothers, for teaching me to look for the magic in life and, indeed, how to spell; Philip Whelan, "Doc," and Sheila Fraser. Milne, for so much advice and love; and last but absolutely not least, Gavrik, my head gardener, hero, and the man of my dreams.